climbingvines
A Collection of Short Stories

Compiled and Edited by Janay Sylvester

Second Edition, 2020

This book was printed with the support of
the Penn Women's Center and
generous donations made to the
Climbing Vines GoFundMe Campaign.

Cover art and design by Ruani Ribe
Additional edits by Victoria Ford

cvines.org

dedication

This book is dedicated to Sharree R. Walls (1991–2019), a 2013 College of Arts and Sciences graduate and Climbing Vines contributor.

Sharree, your story contribution to Climbing Vines is just one of the many ways your exceptional legacy of service lives on. Thank you for lighting the way for future generations of Penn women.

We will continue to tell your story for years to come.

table of contents

"We must always attempt to *lift* as we *climb*."

—Angela Davis

foreword

Climbing Vines is a thought-provoking and thoughtful read. As I poured over the book, with astonishment and glee, I couldn't help but wonder how different and better my own undergraduate experience here would have been if I had contributed to or benefited from such a high-stakes literary endeavor. That it is with us now, when we most need it, is a testament to the vision of its editors, the talent of its writers, and aesthetic urgency of our current political moment.

Professor Salamishah Tillet, C'96
Henry Rutgers Professor of African American and African Studies and Creative Writing at Rutgers University-Newark
Faculty Director of the New Arts Justice Initiative at Express Newark

introduction

In September 2014 one of my dreams came true—The Climbing Vines Collection of Short Stories was published.

Climbing Vines is a project I began working on shortly after graduating from Penn in 2012. The project's aim was simple: to tell the stories of black women who attended the University of Pennsylvania as undergraduates.

After two years of collecting stories and garnering support from so many students, alumnae, and university organizations, it was surreal to see the book in the hands of our guests at the release party in 2014. In the following year almost 400 copies of the book were distributed on and off campus.

Yet with all the work that was done to produce the printed collection, there was still work to be done to ensure that the stories aren't lost, and that we continue to grow the archive for generations to come.

On the sixth anniversary of the book release, I am so thankful to make the book available again, now in print and eBook form, with three new stories covering topics we had yet to explore.

With all of the work, our mission remains the same: to encourage discussion that promotes mental health, and progressive academic and social experiences for black undergraduate women at Penn.

I hope you enjoy the second edition of The Climbing Vines Collection of Short Stories.

Janay Sylvester
Executive Editor

on sisterhood

"Sisterhood *here* is *necessary*."

sister cycles

Penn has been a marker of cycles in my life. As a teenager, I visited campus for two college preparatory programs that led me to apply for admission. I completed my four years here determined to be the life-changing Penn student of lore. After an adventurous journey in the real world, I returned to Penn to serve as an administrator, advising the student body to which I once belonged.

Sitting on the other side of the desk, listening to the challenges and struggles—our favorite word during my tenure—of current students I found myself reflecting on the cycle of Penn womanhood and sisterhood. It is consistent. I was bemused to see that ten years later, we fell into the same valleys and fought the same giants. One of my most treasured mentors, Dr. Herman Beavers, recently remarked to a room full of student leaders that cycles of growth and excitement/attrition and apathy in any institution are to be expected. We could run from them, but we should accept and grow in them. We should never just repeat them. Every round should go higher, higher.

My time at Penn did not make me whole. In many ways, it was a place of wounding. A strange kind of therapy began with my moments of counseling students because they forced me to face my college self in all of her awkwardness. These younger Penn women were trying to be emergent beacons of light for their friends, family, and community. They were performing their success, faking it until they made it, nobly bearing the expectations of black excellence and feminist solidarity while balancing their studies. Or not. My familiarity with this world gave me new eyes, and I saw stories that were not shared with me. These stories, hidden behind "Penn face" and a fresh beat, told of the discomfort of transformation—from the loneliness of the isolation in the cocoon to the pain of wriggling out of constraints into new iterations of self, all the while looking outward and wondering—*does anyone see me?*

I recall, with the requisite twinge of embarrassment, my exuberant 18-year-old self. I was dripping with naïveté and held a wide-eyed wonder that made most people forgive my ignorance. Never having encountered this many black people at once, I was spun round in my curiosity. "You're from where?" "How do you braid your hair like that?" *Why is everyone so damn pretty? Am I pretty? Do I even belong here?* I recall the stares of upperclassmen women when I entered Du Bois, the up-and-down, the side-eye. I smiled and waved. I waited to be noticed, I sat timidly in corners of the lobby. I treaded lightly.

In my first months, I felt more at home at Commons, where my crew from AFAMS (Africana) or PennCAP's pre-freshman program (PFP) would gather for meals. I was lucky to have entered September with friends, insulated from the isolation that can descend upon you. I had a head start on meeting the other brown faces that would be my rocks during my time at the Ivory Tower, which sits no more than five miles from my West Philly home.

From my little pond of happy—the land of "we all know each other"—I could look out onto the rapids of Locust Walk and see the other women, navigating the waters alone with eyes boring into the distance. Did they want to be there? Did they know we were here? I would look to them to offer an opening for conversation, but more often than not my glance would not be met. I played off many an unanswered wave on Locust Walk.

Sisterhood here can be fractured.

By my second semester I could name at least one cause of the fracture. I had a few names actually. Kev, Mike, Jamal—name a trick, they would pull it. Enrolled at Penn, Drexel, Temple, or Villanova—whoever was close and had access to Penn women, also had a story and sometimes a scandal. I had attended a small high school that was much too small for dating. I had no context for the drama I was seeing. I thought dudes only ran stunts in songs. *This happens in real life*?! Relationships were difficult to cultivate and even harder to keep. We fumbled each other's hearts and expectations daily, and in the end the walking wounded still had to go to class, heartbroken, embarrassed, and distracted.

Sophomore year came and went. I partnered with a fellow sophomore with whom I would remain with for the better part of a decade. But the game did not change. Freshman couples-for-life disengaged with the new "crop" of females. Heady with hip-hop, we were too strong to sweat a scrub. Hurt feelings were not displayed. Women blamed women in hushed tones. Dudes scurried around campus, some with our permission, some with our invitation, some due to our resignation. This place is small. It can be lonely. We all understand.

Sisterhood here is a choice.

Summer internships and time abroad provided much needed separation to us weary sophomores. By junior year we were all in the same gang, back in love again. Old couples reconciled, some just forgave each other for that "young boy/young girl" mentality we used to have—as if it were not all of two years ago. Those that could not forget, ignored. We carried on. We looked the new group of freshman girls up and down. We held the sophomores to the shame of their first-year mistakes. Labeled. Stamped. Shunned. Their crises were our jokes. No longer Du Bois-bound; we were high-rise honeys, independent and free. (Prior to the mid-00s, the high rises we restricted to upperclassmen.) Grown.

Junior year was a time of decision-making, a come-to-Jesus moment for career choice, friendship allegiances, and our futures. As much as I had grown intellectually, I found myself stunted in my identity, even though faculty and staff continually poured encouragement into me. Walking through forests of crisp patterned shirts and perfectly coifed executives-elect in Wharton, I felt not only different, but also invisible. Unwanted. Unnecessary. Suffered. Yet somehow, in my loneliness, I found a place of renewal: the arts.

The black student arts community consisted of the African American Arts Alliance (4A), the Inspiration and African Rhythms. In these groups we grew beyond our academic labels into full, creative, thriving human beings. We revealed ourselves to one another and created safe space. Although the time lost being "artsy"—as performer or guest—might otherwise have garnered a better grade in our classes, it was time invested into our souls and therefore time well spent.

Sisterhood here is beautiful.

My junior spring semester, 4A performed Ntozake Shange's *for colored girls who have considered suicide/when the rainbow is enuf* three times over the course of a weekend for audiences of sister friends, families, current and former lovers, and the community. We danced for each other. We cried for ourselves. This joining of women from all class years changed us. The diversity of our sister experience was expressed in the choreopoem and it allowed us to stop, for just a moment, and publicly love each other fiercely.

Sisterhood here has its responsibilities.

My senior year was one of worry, wear, and general resignation. We were pendulums that would swing between "I'm going to miss you so much," to "I cannot wait until I don't have to see you anymore!"

That spring, in the midst of the headiness of impending graduation, Ntozake Shange came to campus. She spoke to a packed Multi-Purpose Room of Du Bois, full of Penn women and community members staring deep into her scarlet mouth, waiting for her wisdom to heal us. I was late to the event and looking out from a back row; I only caught the Q&A session. The exact question escapes me, but the answer I will never forget:

"Do not idolize me. I am not an idol. I wrote this, yes, but I am no better than you."

I was stunned. I would venture to say that everyone in the room was, as well. Here was this woman prophet, telling us that she was human, that we were somehow like her. Her tone was angry—as if we should never even dare to think less of ourselves. She challenged us to wholeness, to greatness, to humility, to completion. She told us not to waste time in worshiping others, but to invest time in becoming ourselves. There I was, struggling to just get out of Penn, and she was demanding my best performance—and presence in the moment.

The final weeks of Penn are celebratory for most, but mine were fraught with worry. I did not exit with a job offer. I left in debt to multiple sources. Still, I felt compelled to remain in the moment. I shared all I could with underclassmen. I spent as much time as I could with faculty and staff I loved. I went to places on campus I had never been. I was at the end of my journey, and it was time to give—not just take.

This last cycle of giving back and sharing truth never stops. It is the most rewarding stage because in it you realize how much you were able to create with what was poured into you. This stage is how we grow *Higher! Higher!* But you cannot get here without going through all the others.

Our sister cycles have taught me that the worst person we can idolize is our future self. We owe ourselves the kindness and compassion to love ourselves where we are. Each phase has purpose. I resist the urge to pump up a downtrodden sophomore, because her valley is her place of strengthening. I do not doubt the ebullience of a freshman; she has a right to her happiness. I work hard to listen to the dreams of a junior, because that moment is the founding of her identity, deserving of reverence and support. I still look forward to offering hugs to the departing seniors, knowing their lives' work will eclipse their expectations in ways they could never fathom. I support those who find the straight path of four years to be difficult or circumstantially impossible, who need the confirmation that they too are Penn women. As I look back on the cycles of my Penn experience, I can assert:

Sisterhood here is necessary.

"Remember *those* nights?"

letter to my girls

January 12, 2014

Dear friends,

I do not think I tell any of you enough how much I appreciate you.

Despite the physical or emotional distance that has come between us over the years since we graduated, I am reassured by the fact that all of you are a video chat, phone call, train ride, plane ride, or text message away.

Forgive me for sharing this, but the thought just occurred to me that we're a couple years shy of it being a decade since we first met at Penn. I know, I know. Most of you don't want to hear this, especially given the amount of times I've heard the apocalyptic phrase "other side of 25" coming from many of your mouths.

But we all know what the opposite of growing old is, and none of us want any parts of that, so we might as well accept our waning youth and get on with it.

Sorry. You all know that I'm dramatic. And on top of that, I'm a huge sap so writing to you is making me feel wistful as I reminisce about the beginnings of our friendships.

Do you remember what it felt like to be dropped off on a campus full of strangers? I was cool about it for a couple weeks, but I can admit that one day I cried a little while writing an entry in my journal about having to establish a whole new life for myself five hours away from a familiar place and familiar faces. Thankfully it didn't take long for you ladies to step into my life.

We met in awkward extracurricular groups or at raucous parties where a sympathetic face offered much respite. We met in classrooms or over dinner in dining halls. We met in dorm rooms or in noticeable freshman droves loitering on Locust Walk during NSO. Some of you were kind enough to share your CrackDonald's fries in drunken peace offerings of sorts after long nights of the kind of partying you do when you're no longer obligated to answer to any authority figure but God.

Remember those nights? We were impervious to fear and cold as we explored Philadelphia far outside of the Penn bubble in our mini-skirted glory. I laugh from my gut every time I remember the cab driver kicking us out and leaving us on a barren North Philadelphia corner because we stuffed ourselves sardine-like into his cab. Of course, it wasn't too funny when it happened.

We would dance until inhumane pain radiated from the soles of our feet. The pain was often worth the opportunity to let the bass at sweatbox parties mute our thoughts of assignments and exams, or the rush of being grabbed by the cutie you had your eye on all night to dance in a corner under the watchful eyes of your friends. Thanks for always looking out for me, and giving me shoulders to lean on during the torturous nights we hobbled home.

Boys. We shared laughs and tears over these creatures in equal measure. We rejoiced when someone found a boyfriend or had a great date, a real date that did not involve "watching a movie" in his dorm or apartment. We always reacted with the perfect amount of vitriol whenever a dude messed up.

Thank you for helping me steal my card from He Who Shall Not Be Named's room so I could cut it up into confetti to help assuage the hatred I felt when he picked her and not me.

Whenever people ask me about my college days I jest that I miss socializing at school, not the schoolwork. But that's not entirely true because without the schoolwork we would not have had those precious moments of bonding under duress.

We used to cut up in the computer lab. There was this peculiar giddy feeling that came over us during the witching hour when our bodies craved sleep, but our minds told us that a good grade was of paramount importance. Caffeine, laughter, and sugar got us through it.

That academic pressure was something else. When I realized that the pre-med path was only going to lead me to hell, you ladies talked me through it and helped me re-discover the joy that learning brings. I looked forward to the classes that I took with some of you, and relished the academic discussions we had outside of the classroom.

Thank you for being a free, psychological service when life overwhelmed me and I did not have the wherewithal to seek professional help.

Of course our friendships also went through their share of trying times, but when you fight like family, you love like family. Recovering from disagreements made our friendships richer.

No one told us that our twenties would be so mind/spirit/soul-shifting in the best and worst of ways. But reflecting on the fun we had reminds me that there are still so many more beautiful memories ahead.

Love,

Janday

identity & belonging

"During my time at Penn, I had little idea of *who I was* and was not certain of *who I wasn't.*"

the ramblings of me

"Are you black?" "How come I've never seen you before?" "I think I know your face, what's your name again?"

Countless times I have been passed over, unacknowledged. Someone else's friend/sister/cousin. Never my own person.

During my time at Penn, I had little idea of who I was and was not certain of who I wasn't. I did know that how I was, was not accepted by everyone. I was the girl who loved *The Lord of the Rings*, who didn't mind staying in on a Saturday night, who had a few really close friends and a lot of acquaintances, who liked to break it down once in a while. But at school, I felt like I needed to be someone else. I couldn't be that person because that person wasn't accepted.

Black Penn saw me as an anomaly, someone who stood out from the norm. I didn't do what everyone else did. I didn't hook up with anyone with two legs who paid me attention. I didn't go out from Thursday to Saturday, smoking weed, drinking up a storm, or partying my ass off all the time. White/Asian Penn thought I was interesting. Interested in some of the same things, but black. Honestly, that's it. I was black and there existed another barrier there that I couldn't break down.

I was "un-label-able" (I made up my own word I know, but I was). I was the cute girl, who never really fit in, and I still don't really fit in. It took me going away, going abroad, to really understand that idea. That it was okay for me to be who I was, who I am, and that I didn't have to fit someone else's mold of what it meant to be a "black person" in Black Penn or to be an "oreo" in White/Asian Penn.

I am the woman who loves *The Lord of the Rings*, who doesn't mind staying in on a Saturday night, who has a few really close friends and a lot of acquaintances, and who likes to break it down once in a while. I'm me, and it took going to Penn and going abroad to really find that out. And I'm grateful that I did.

"Africana was the *spark* I needed to make me realize
the *strength* Black Penn possessed."

the black hole

Growing up, I've always felt "too white to be black" and "too black to be white." Yet even though I never felt like I belonged in a specific category, I somehow gained some sort of "Duality Superpower." Although I didn't feel 100 percent comfortable in any type of situation, I at least felt like I could survive in either of them.

Once accepted into Penn, I didn't know which direction I wanted to go in or who I wanted to be; better yet, I didn't know who I wanted other people to think I was. For some reason, I thought I needed to pick a side. Almost like my "Duality Superpower" needed to become null-in-void. Did I want to be Black Jacqueline or White Jacqueline? What was going to be easier for me? What would people believe? The first moment of truth came in May 2009 when I was invited to attend the Africana Summer Institute. If anything, I should've been thrilled that I could stay in dormitories, eat in dining halls, take classes, meet professors, and make friends all before my freshman year. However, that was not the case for me—in reality, I didn't even want to go. Looking back on the situation, I can admit that I was too worried about what other people thought about me. I didn't want to get sucked into what I called "the Black Hole." I didn't want to be friends with only black people and I didn't want to participate in only "black" activities. I thought by participating in the program, that was what was going to happen. After reflecting on my initial reasoning for rejecting the Africana Summer Institute, I feel like a coward for wanting to reject my blackness. I feel guilty for thinking there was something wrong with surrounding myself with powerful black students and professors. I think I was trying to prove something to all those people in high school that thought I was only going to get somewhere because I was black. I wanted to prove those students that used to have debates in the middle of calculus class about whether or not I was admitted into Penn because I was black, wrong. I wanted to show them that I could operate with everyone else and not be the best black person for the job, but I could be the best person period. So I thought that I could redefine my identity by removing myself from Black Penn before I even started officially attending the University.

If my mother didn't tell me to get my act together and enjoy the opportunities Africana had to offer, I know for a fact that my Penn experience would've been much different. Africana was the spark I needed to make me realize the strength Black Penn possessed. Fortunately, I decided to embrace it instead of running away from it. I elected to create my own path and choose activities that I found enjoyable, not activities that made me either black or white. Alpha Kappa Alpha Sorority, Incorporated. Quaker Girls Dance team. Co-President of the Multicultural Greek Council. Fisher Hassenfeld Resident Assistant. Onyx Senior Honor Society. Big Brothers Big Sisters. Assistant Manager of the Sprint Football team. Black Student League peer mentor. Those were MY activities, and I joined them because that was what I wanted. I began making decisions for myself instead of everyone else for once.

Now that I've graduated, I can truly say that I'm ecstatic with my involvement in the activities that I chose. I think I chose a perfect blend while still staying true to myself. Penn has helped me become a better me—I know now that it's not about conforming to a specific standard, it's about finding that inner strength and passion that allows me to construct my own meaning and identity of my life. I finally feel a little more comfortable in my own skin. And at this point, I just want to be too Jacqueline to be anybody else.

"I wasn't an insider, but I was definitely *welcome in either sphere.*"

not miss black penn

I first set foot on Penn's campus as a high school sophomore, on a whirlwind college tour organized by my college counselors. Every spring break, they, along with the deans of students and a handful of teacher-chaperones, shepherded forty of us high school girls through twenty-five east coast college campuses. We hit every top-ranked school from Winston-Salem to Providence, in less than a week. By day three and college eight, all of the campuses were running together. I'd fallen in love with a couple, charmed by Columbia and Duke, mostly because the tour guides at those schools were chipper recent graduates of my high school. They were girls who were just like me, who seemed happy and popular and settled after only a semester and a half away from Los Angeles and high school and their lives for the eighteen years prior.

We visited Penn on one of the first warm days of the season. No one, not even the most critical Quaker, can deny the romance of Locust Walk in the springtime—trees all abloom and students smiling, wearing shorts for the first time that season, grateful that winter had finally loosened its grip. Our tour guide that day was an alum of my high school, Ashley, a super-cute black girl whose mom was friends with my mom, and who was a dancer in the high school dance company I'd go on to join the next school year. Though she was three years older and we weren't necessarily friends, our high school was too tiny and had too few black girls for us not to know every intimate detail about the other. She led our group down the Walk, pointed out Van Pelt and Fisher Fine Arts and Logan Hall and spoke of the foulness of dining hall food and snow and Penn boys and the mouse visitors she had in her dorm room in Du Bois College House. She didn't really like Penn, it seemed, but I did.

Two years later, she was one of the first people I talked to when I got in. A rising senior then, I knew Ashley would look out for me. She told me where to get my hair done ("Shavonne's so sweet and the best stylist"), which all-you-can-eat Indian buffet was best, which boys to avoid, and where to live freshman year. "Don't live in Du Bois," she told me. "Live in the Quad. You'll make black friends wherever you live, but if you live in

Du Bois it's going to be really hard for you to make any friends who aren't black." The thought of only having friends of one race was completely foreign to me. My closest high school friends could easily have been featured in a Benetton ad—black girls, white girls, Asian girls—our charm and our bond was that we came from different backgrounds. Those girls are still some of my closest friends.

I took Ashley's advice. When asked to rank my choices for college houses, I ranked Du Bois fifth, after the three college houses in the Quad and Hill, and waited to see where I'd end up. That summer after senior year, when the pamphlets arrived promoting Africana and PFP and other pre-freshman programs, I ignored them. I didn't want to spend my last summer in Los Angeles away from my friends and my family and the city that I thought might never be my home again, even if it was only for a week.

My freshman year roommate was a nerdy Chinese girl from Cherry Hill, New Jersey, who spent almost all of her weekends at home with her parents. One of the first nights in our new room, Grace called her mom, near tears, complaining that her roommate wasn't Asian. I was sitting on my bed, approximately six inches from her and while I was slightly offended and really amused, I understood where she was coming from. No one on our hall was like her. No one on our hall was like me either.

The residents on my freshman hall were from super-white suburbs in New Jersey, New York, and Pennsylvania. A half-Belizean, half-white girl from Harrisburg, Pennsylvania, lived two doors down. At the beginning, I gravitated toward her, the only other brown girl on the hall, but I soon learned that she was much more similar to the other girls on our floor, sweet, funny white girls from other Tri-state suburban towns, who wore lots of eyeliner and flat-ironed their hair every morning before class. I was the only black girl on the hall, forced to explain why I wrapped my hair at night, or didn't feel particularly moved to go to some frat party where I'd be forced to watch drunken coeds bopping off-beat to "Sweet Caroline" or "Pour Some Sugar on Me." Those first couple of weeks, when all my hall-mates and I travelled, en masse, to the cafeteria or to some orientation or another, I'd see groups of black students doing the same. We might smile at each other, but I was always self-conscious, acutely aware of how it looked to be the only black person in a sea of white faces. Did they think I didn't want to make black friends—that I was trying to pass or something? I liked my new friends from my hall, but I was determined to make some who were more like me.

Not only was I the only black girl on the hall, I was also the only city mouse, drawn to the other city kids I met. At Commons one afternoon, I saw a cute, well-dressed black girl, piling salad fixings onto a plate. It was still early enough in the school year to spark up conversations with random people, so I pounced. She was from New York, born and raised in Brooklyn. She also lived in the Quad, a few floors above me, and she hadn't done Africana or PFP either, but her roommate was black. We bonded. Both of us had a diverse group of friends back home and felt a little like outsiders to the people who'd done those pre-freshman programs and lived in Du Bois. We weren't apart of "Black Penn."

There were a few cute black guys from Los Angeles a couple classes above me. I knew some of them from home; my mom, a pediatrician, had been the doctor of a few. One of my high school friends, another black girl, had gotten close to them and would invite me along when they went to MarBar or had a pregame at one of their off-campus apartments. It was nice, feeling like I was a part of some community of black people, even if I didn't feel particularly connected to it. They were "cool," partied hard, spent a lot of money and even though they were always nice to me, I didn't feel like I was one of them either. I think I was a little too square.

When freshman year ended, I had made a few really close girlfriends, some from my hall, some that I'd met in class or in CityStep, and the one that I'd met in that salad line at Commons. When I came back for sophomore year, though, I was determined to make more friends who felt like me. I had done theater all through high school and decided to try out for the 4A production, a monologue show. Those first few rehearsals were hard. Most of the cast already knew each other, had lived in Du Bois together, been in BWUA or NSBE together, or done another production the semester before.

One of the first days a cast member, a football player from New York, came up to me—"Who are you?" he asked, not in a particularly friendly way. "I've never even seen you before." I told him my stats, name, city of origin, major. He wasn't impressed.

As the weeks wore on, the long hours spent rehearsing allowed all of us to bond. I, along with three other girls in the production, were always gossiping, swapping Penn "dating" war stories, gabbing about our crushes and our friends back home, asking and offering advice. It was the first time I felt like I actually belonged somewhere in the Black Penn landscape. Once we'd all gotten to know each other, one girl (now, one of my closest friends) told me, "I'd seen you around campus and thought that you seemed uppity and only had white friends or rich friends, but you aren't actually like that." I heard a lot of comments like that, as I navigated through Black Penn over the course of my time there. People were surprised that I wasn't a snob or a bitch or a self-hater, because I had lived in the quad and spent a lot of time with my white friends. I made more black friends, in 4A, in CityStep, in class, in Onyx, but I was never going to be a part of that Black Penn inner sanctum.

I didn't mind being on the periphery. It allowed me the fluidity to travel back and forth between a lot of different circles, but it meant I wasn't really a part of any. I had some really close friends from a couple different groups, but I didn't have one clique of my own, I was a floater. My senior year, during rehearsals for my final 4A show, one of my castmates, a junior guy, told me something that I'd never forget. "You are the only black person I know who is equally comfortable with your white friends and your black friends." I hadn't realized it until he said it, but he was right. I wasn't an insider, but I was definitely welcome in either sphere.

If I could do it over again, I wouldn't change much. I might have done Africana—that may have made things a little easier—but I don't regret taking Ashley's advice about housing. A girl who lived across the hall from me freshman year, one of the eye-liner-wearing white girls, is my best friend from Penn and has been my roommate since sophomore year of college. If I'd lived in Du Bois, I'm almost certain we would have never met. Being outside of that Black Penn community forced me to try to carve out some space there for myself. Who knows if I would have joined 4A, made all the effort to find amazing black friends, whom I continue to love, if I'd already felt like I was a part of the community. My group of post-college friends looks a lot like my group of high school friends. We're very "multi-culti," or as we like to call ourselves, "wild rice." I can't imagine it any other way.

"I 'othered' myself. I chose which parts of my identity mattered more than others."

d.i.y.: draft your own story

"Timidity makes a person modest. It makes him or her say, 'I'm not worthy of being written up in the record of deeds in heaven or on earth.' Timidity keeps people from their good. They are afraid to say, 'Yes, I deserve it.'" —Maya Angelou

Unsure, doubtful, small. I never used these words to describe myself out loud, but they had a silent presence that filled up too much room for improvements. Nothing around me, even success, could remove the fear I didn't want to face.

I spent four years of high school in rigorous honors and AP classes while involved in extracurricular activities including athletics, dance, theater and speech team, student council, and honor societies. I had a near perfect GPA, except for the semesterly blemishes from math classes. My senior portrait even displayed in the hallway as one of our school district's top students. You could say that I was a model student, except I didn't feel like one.

As early as I can remember, administrators and teachers questioned my academic abilities. For many years in elementary school, school administrators placed me in remedial reading while my teachers placed me in advanced reading classes and projects. In the years transitioning from elementary and middle school, I had near-perfect math homework and test grades, but moved into advanced math two years later. The list goes on. Instead of growing confident in my academic abilities based on my performance, mixed expectations from adults confused my perception of my capacity to learn.

By March 2009, I was accepted into an overwhelming majority of the fifteen schools I applied to. Of those acceptances, I chose Penn after visiting during their multicultural scholars weekend. In the months that passed between choosing to go to Penn, graduation, and the summer, I was filled with anxiety. I thought Penn made a mistake, and I made a mistake thinking that I could go to a school like Penn. I had serious reservations about my ability to continue to perform well academically and fit in socially, based on my presumptions about how I differed from a typical Ivy League student. I was sure they would know I wasn't as smart as them, and perhaps believe my race helped me in admissions.

"Modesty is a learned adaptation." —Maya Angelou

I began my Penn tenure at a three-day leadership pre-orientation program, PENNacle. Together, with about sixty other freshmen, we challenged ourselves to ask and answer tough questions and spent most of our time socializing. By the end of the three days we just knew the to-be-elected freshman class president was in our midst. People began throwing around names and somehow my name came up. I was shocked after only three days of knowing me, *Penn* classmates wanted to vote for me as president? This felt like an alternate universe. How could my new classmates think more highly of me than I thought of myself?

There was no room for modesty at Penn. I was surrounded by intelligent and ambitious peers, who only assumed I was just as intelligent and ambitious as they were. There was no room for thinking small. Every quad "study" session, dining hall meal, and leadership experience pushed me to dream and share ambitious goals. While these goals were my own thoughts, I remember feeling like I created goals in an effort to "fit in" rather than actually believing that one day I could achieve any of them.

The initial excitement of being a part of such an accomplished group of 18- to 22-year-olds quickly transformed into a sense of pressure to perform, wherein I did not have the confidence to follow through on my newly-scaled ambitions. After all, I still never resolved my lack of acknowledgement and confidence in my abilities. Being so close to peers who owned their abilities to achieve, who came from mostly privileged and affirmed backgrounds, energized thoughts that I didn't quite belong. Despite blossoming friendships and "good" grades, I didn't allow myself to feel a part of the Penn privileged society.

I "othered" myself. I chose which parts of my identity mattered more than others. I considered my traits that were similar to my peers to be external while holding those that separated me deeply internal. Along with believing that I wasn't "that" smart, I questioned what I deserved as a person from an unstable economic background. To me, it didn't matter how hard I worked or how I excelled, I knew it didn't entitle me to anything. After all, I always looked up to my parents as highly intelligent and hard-working individuals—but those traits did not guarantee career or financial success. In moments of deep reflection, I would ask myself: "So what if I have good grades, friends, and developing goals?" I became anxious to position myself for success, but I struggled to determine what would be my bridge to success if it wasn't effort. How would I feel relief that my outcomes could match my level of input?

If there is one theme I learned as an urban studies major—dissecting how society works—is that narratives are powerful. Narratives determine what people think about their neighbors, strangers, the economy, the government, the environment, and the list goes on. Even more pressing than the narrative itself is the understanding that the narrative is always constructed. In unraveling how society is constructed through narratives that are fact, fiction, and/or irrelevant, I realized I repeated societal and external narratives internally and was too timid to construct my own narrative.

After four years of efforts in the form of ambition, I've learned the bridge to success is to have the courage to write my own story and place it on repeat until I accept it. And after writing many papers where I "stretched" my ideas, extending them beyond my own genuine belief for the sake of reaching a page limit, I've learned that my story can be credibly delusional in the direction of ambition as well. Besides, why not? It works everywhere else!

diversity in the classroom

"I, as a *black woman*, am both of these minority identities combined; I'm essentially *a unicorn*."

the unicorn

"It'll be hard, but you can do it." "You can do whatever you set your mind to." "You just have to keep it pushing." I've heard and repeated all of these phrases—and others like them—to myself far too many times to count. I usually use them to help brush the dirt off my shoulders and pick myself back up after a particularly tough exam or significant setback. They worked pretty well at first, and helped refocus me on doing better next time. That is until next time came and I found myself on the floor, or other side of the curve rather, yet again. It was during these frequent stumbles and sometimes even hard falls that I looked around to see who was standing around me and tried to find familiar faces among the crowd. I found none.

Women are significantly underrepresented in STEM (science, technology, engineering, and mathematics) fields; people of color are even more woefully absent. I, as a black woman, am both of these minority identities combined; I'm essentially a unicorn. I am a biology major with a neurobiology concentration and chemistry minor in the College here at Penn. I am also pre-med with hopes of going to medical school and eventually becoming a neurosurgeon. While it can be very empowering to stand as a tangible contradiction to stereotypes, to be living proof that it is possible, it is also incredibly isolating and lonely. It gets harder and harder to tell myself that I can do it and to "keep it pushing" when there is no one around me to look up to that has.

How can I believe that it is not only possible, but also likely that I will succeed as a biology major and future part of the STEM workforce when in my nearly three years here at Penn, I have never once had a black male or female science professor? As a biology major, I have been trained to think like a scientist and utilize the scientific method. The scientific method follows as such:

1. *Ask a question*: Can I succeed as a biology major here at Penn?

2. *Do background research*: There are no black women in the biology

department here a Penn to serve as evidence that it is possible to be successful in the long term. There aren't, to the best of my knowledge at least, any black female biology TAs that would serve as evidence that is it possible in the short term. There are very few black males and/or females in biology classes (I can usually count them on one hand).

3. *Hypothesis*: Based on the background research, I would predict that it would be very hard, if not impossible for me to succeed and thrive as a biology major here at Penn.

4. *Experiment*: Major in biology. See how it goes, what difficulties and setbacks I face, and if my hypothesis will be proven correct. Try to explain the observations I made while doing my background research: why are there so few black women (and black men) in the biology department and in STEM fields in general?

5. *Results*: Being a biology major, or any STEM major in general, is very difficult. The material is dense, complex, and often voluminous. Dutifully going to class and recitation and doing all the assigned readings and assignments is challenging due to time and human constraints, like the need to sleep and eat, and by no means guarantees one an A.

6. *Conclusion*: To be announced.

While I am still in the results process of the scientific method, for all intents and purposes, the conclusion is a forgone one. There are many reasons why there are so few women, and even fewer women of color, in the biology department at Penn and in STEM fields in general; I want to focus on one. I want to focus on the importance of having role models/mentors/reference points that look like me—the importance of being able to look to someone who shares and understands the interlocking systems of oppression that come together to constitute my marginalized reality, someone who, despite all this, was able to succeed and thrive. The presence of this person, this black female biology professor or TA is inherently valuable in that it is implicit confirmation and validation of my aspirations and dreams. These are the familiar faces in the crowd that I seek for inspiration and motivation when I stumble and fall. These are the familiar faces in the crowd that I seek for comfort and support when I am the singular representative—or one of very few—of the black population in my biology classes as I often am. How can I convince myself and tell myself that I can do it, when I have little to no proof that anyone else has done it before me and that it is possible?

I can still remember the feeling of shock and incredulity I felt when sitting in my biochemistry class at the beginning of this spring semester and my white male professor asked us all to look around and remarked, in all seriousness, that the class was very diverse this year. I thought it was some kind of sharply sardonic joke since there were all of about seven black students (male and female) in a nearly two-hundred-student class. Doing the math, we weren't even 0.1 percent of the largely white and/or Asian class. I was hopeful but unsurprised when I walked into my upper level neurobiology class this semester and was the only black student. Judging by the mildly puzzled looks on their faces, it took the other students some time to realize that I didn't accidently stumble into the wrong room and was in fact part of the class. It is in situations like this that I am acutely aware of my unicorn status and realize that I inevitably have to take on the responsibility of representing all other black women. I perform this duty as well as I am capable and try to defend my, as well as other black women's, right to be in these STEM spaces by being a good, alert student and asking good questions.

In more difficult times, however, when I perform more poorly than expected on an exam or get rejected from an internship I had applied to, or can't comfortably confide in the majority of my peers, I seek out these anchors and tangible sources of motivation and inspiration. Except there are none to be found. Constantly coming up empty makes the process of dusting myself off and getting back up that much harder. This absence of black women in the biology department speaks volumes, as does the minuscule population of black students in biology classes. The implicit message being that this isn't a field meant for you, it does not serve or accommodate your kind. I would argue from my experience that this implicit message is a significant contributor to why there are so few black women not only in the Penn biology department, but in STEM fields in general.

As human beings we are constantly seeking the validation of ourselves, of our hopes and dreams and desires. We have evolved to spend our time pursing activities and endeavors that give us positive feedback (things that we are good at and can reap benefits from), and when we find that an activity is difficult and gives us negative feedback (things that we have to work hard for in order to reap benefits) we need compelling reasons to continue investing precious and limited resources like time and energy into these activities. One compelling reason would be a reasonable chance and concrete evidence that we might actually succeed in this endeavor. Without this kind of positive impetus, it becomes more and more unlikely that one will continue to stay on this difficult path. There is something inherently valuable in being able to see a tangible manifestation of my future self. It would motivate me to keep working towards that future despite the difficulties I face now. I am striving to be that person for others that will follow, to make their path a bit less bumpy and rough.

building a business

"During my time at Penn my development as a *photographer* and as a *businesswoman* came together."

phases of photography

This oral story was transcribed and edited for length.

What did my journey through photography look like?

I would say that I have been fascinated with cameras since a really early age. I was photographing on my mom's little Nikon Coolpix when I was in the fourth or fifth grade. Back then, I was also in the yearbook club, which meant I could check out a camera from the school library and document the day-to-day activities during my various classes.

Fast forward to eighth grade when I somehow managed to convince my mom to buy me a proper DSLR camera. I remember what she said to me once we had gotten into the car: "This is an investment." Those words have stuck with me since. Nothing comes without hard work and effort. I think those words had long-term effects on the kinds of photographic work I would go on to pursue.

In high school, I spent a lot of time shooting everything and anything I could. Every day I had my camera—I was still on the yearbook committee—and by my senior year I had taken the majority of my school's photos. The pictures themselves weren't that great, but that's fine. I think that's one big part of development that people want to disregard. It's the part that's not so glamorous. I think those years were very formative. I had all the time in the world to run around and just take pictures of so many different things. I also had the privilege of taking a few photography/art classes with my wonderful high school IB (International Baccalaureate) Art teacher. Gradually, this started to inform what I like to take pictures of, what I don't like taking pictures of, what the best lighting situations were, etc. That was phase one, the introduction to my time in photography.

And then I got to Penn. The first semester was so difficult for me I didn't even pick up my camera once. I didn't bring my camera out until my second semester, for a D9 MLK vigil. I just thought, I'm a little stressed and want to take a deep breath…everyone will be there…the candles at night might be cool. I posted them to Facebook and soon a whole lot of people were liking, commenting, and sharing. I think that was the start of my time shooting at Penn, when I was really just getting a handle on taking pictures for others.

I believe mentorship is key. There were two people in particular that really influenced my path to photography while at Penn. Tim Lee, who at the time was photographing for our Fall 2015 Strictly Funk show (I was in the Strictly Funk Dance Company, a hip-hop and contemporary dance group on Penn's campus). When I saw him shooting, I immediately went over to find out what he was doing, what kinds of ideas he had. Tim was the kind of guy who really did appreciate teaching; he helped me to understand editing, what my camera settings should be based on the situation, etc. He even set me up with little gigs around campus. Soon, more and more people were asking me to shoot and by junior year, I was photographing a majority of the major shows and performances for Penn. Thanks to Tim's teachings, I worked hard to develop my expertise in performance photography. I really began to hone my craft as a photographer who could handle all different kinds of light, and that is very key to photography.

The other person that really influenced my career was Collin Williams. When I was at Penn as a sophomore, he was a GA at Hill College House and a grad student pursuing his PhD. But at the same time, he was also hosting club events all around Philly. He saw me photographing around campus and asked me to shoot one of his events. Soon after that I became his go-to photographer. At events, it's your job to take the emotion, the feeling, the vibe of the event and bring it forth. So I'd say that was phase two. Having those events available to me as a sophomore were really eye-opening because I was entering into a world that most people my age did not have access to. And thanks to the work, I was being exposed to all sorts of new situations, and more importantly, new people. I didn't realize, but I was gaining access into a proper "network" thanks to Collin.

During my time at Penn my development as a photographer and as a businesswoman came together. By the time I got to my senior year, I realized I was burnt out from all the events. I felt like I was getting used for this, that, and the other like a gun for hire. It would be hard for me to price myself sometimes because people would say, "Oh well, I'll ask somebody else who's cheaper." If you really want to make your passion into a career, you can't ever be in a space where somebody else can determine your value. I had to start to differentiate myself—I asked, *Who am I? Who am I as an artist, as a photographer? What is it that I want to do and how can I price myself based off those kinds of things?*

Enter phase three… becoming a documentary photographer. Or rather, a visual storyteller. I realized that I wanted to tell stories, and I wanted to tell them with as few words as possible. I want my work to be able to stand all on its own. You look at the image, and you're hit with a barrage of ideas, of visual cues, of things that you thought you knew that have now been turned on their heads. That is what I want you to see when you look at one of my photos.

During my junior year I decided I was going to take advantage of Penn's ample resources—that's another tip to anyone looking to do what they want at Penn—there's plenty of money, so much money that they're trying to spend on you. I ended up going to Chicago for the summer and found a documentary project where I photographed and interviewed black men around the city. I was attempting to explore what gets a black man out of bed every morning in a country that sees so little value in them. To understand this I asked more than 50 subjects the question, "What is your biggest fear?"

That summer I also realized the importance of having a platform on which to tell your story. Who is promoting your vision? What is the platform—the stage on which you are touting your stories to your readers? Exposure is important. You may not have the resources to be seen, so it's about finding the people who can promote you in that way. And that's what happened. I ended up linking with this guy who ran a magazine, an incredible photographer, creative, and writer. His name is Felton Kizer, and he loved the idea that I was working on for the summer. I remember us sitting outside one of the local Starbucks when he said, "So why don't we have an exhibition this winter?" I was flabbergasted and mostly in disbelief. And yet by January 7, 2017, I had returned to Chicago for my first solo exhibition. This wasn't in Philly or anywhere near Penn and yet somehow the place was packed all night. I think that just shows the power of having a proper stage.

From then on, I realized that having those kinds of people behind you—the ones that you really vibe and connect with, who want to see your vision thrive and vice versa—those are the people you keep around you. With photography, I've been able to develop and grow because I focus on the people who need their stories told. I'm hoping that people will continue to branch out of their comfort zones when it comes to working with me. I appreciate those that really understand what it is that I'm trying to say. I am in the business of changing perception because perception is 100%. Period.

I am actually getting myself ready to move to Ghana, West Africa, for the next few months. I'll be developing my documentary photography out there, as well as expanding on my own personal journey as a Ghanaian woman raised in the U.S.

I'm off to find the next set of stories.

community

"In the *face of adversity* and threats against our friends' lives, we came together to *support one another.*"

who do we turn to?

November 11, 2016. It feels so long ago when I write the date out, but I remember the emotions and fear I experienced like it was yesterday. I'm usually pretty good pretending like everything's okay at school when I call my mom. However, this was the first time I had ever called my mom with discernable fear in my voice. It was the first time I ever heard her fear for my safety in her voice. It was the first time ever that I can remember my mom picking up the phone and calling my school to find out what was going on. Later, they told her that if I felt unsafe, I should "go back home" to New York for the weekend, as if it was that easy or if that solved the larger problem black students were facing as a whole on campus. It was the first time I was scared to walk from work back to my dorm room in Du Bois College House. And it was the first time I had ever seen the black community mobilize and truly come together to protect one another, putting our differences aside even if it was just for a short time.

Just before this so-called GroupMe incident, on November 8, 2016, the "orange man" was elected as the forty-fifth president of the United States. He was elected not by popular vote, but by the Electoral College. Being in Du Bois College House that night watching the election in the MPR, you could feel a wave of sadness overtake the room when we realized that the orange man was about to become the orange president. We knew that with this new administration, many of our family members, close friends, and even ourselves could have rights stripped away. Some of us know DACA recipients personally. Some of us come from families that need government assistance to stay afloat. Almost all of us understood that the increased police presence number 45 was vouching for in low-income communities could mean more of our family and friends being shipped off to prisons. That night, the people of Du Bois prayed together, hugged one another, and wiped each other's tears, telling each other that everything would be okay even though we couldn't be sure that it would be. Outside of Du Bois, I remember stepping out of the dorm and hearing cheering and shouting coming from the windows of other buildings on campus and that's when my initial feelings of dread and worry about what was to come for marginalized students on this campus began.

Fast forward to November 11, 2016. It was a Friday and that semester I worked the majority of my Fridays at my work-study job on the corner of 37th and Chestnut Street. Around noon, I remember checking my phone and seeing that the Students Organizing for Unity and Liberation (SOUL) GroupMe was blowing up. I opened the messages, and my heart dropped. I found screenshots of ugly, racist, and violent messages from a GroupMe chat named "Mud Men" that many of our black brothers and sisters from the Class of 2020 were added to that morning by an unknown person. There were calendar events within the chat for daily lynchings; white members of the group spewed the word nigger; and there were racist and offensive images of black men in this chat, portraying them as ugly criminals. I was a sophomore at the time, so I personally was not added to the Mud Men GroupMe, but many of my friends in the freshman class were. We all understood that though it was only freshman who were added to this GroupMe, this was an attack on the entire black community at the University of Pennsylvania.

Many of us, like myself, went into defense mode to protect our freshman friends. But we also feared for our own safety because we doubted that if there were a lynching on campus, the perpetrators would care to find out what year the person was in school to ensure they were a freshman— they just cared if the person was black. Since I was at work while this was blowing up, I felt helpless. I couldn't make myself available to make sure that people weren't walking alone on campus. I couldn't wipe anyone's tears. And I also couldn't find a community of support at the time the news was developing. As the messages flooded in, I told my supervisor that there were threats of lynching against black students on campus. For context, my supervisor is a Chinese woman who immigrated to the States to pursue higher education. She is a sweet woman, but by no means does she understand the racial dynamics in the U.S. When I told her that I was scared for my safety, she rubbed my shoulders, told me it was going to be okay, and kept going about her day. At that moment, I understood that no one but my fellow Black Penn classmates would be able to understand what I was feeling and be able to help me get through it.

When I got off work, I heard that all black students were gathering in a sort of town hall to make sure each of us knew the others were safe and to also talk through our emotions. I rushed over to the Rodin College House basement, which was packed past maximum capacity by the time I got there. Penn police and security were in the building trying to tell us that we needed to relocate because we were over capacity, but no one was trying to hear that. The trauma we were trying to grapple with? No one cared about a room's "maximum capacity." In that room, I saw people openly cry, hug each other, and love one another. We did end up having to move but were able to secure the MBA Café in the Huntsman building, which was a bigger space and forum to talk. To our surprise, President Amy Gutmann showed up, offered her condolences, and we were able to tell her to her face exactly what we needed from the institution in response to this GroupMe incident.

The conversations occurring in that room were probably some of the most supportive that I have ever heard happen among Black Penn students, period. The only comparable instance is that night in Du Bois MPR after the orange president was elected. I think a lot of people like to pretend that Black Penn is always this super supportive space where everyone is accepted, and we all love each other, but that's far from the case. The only time all our differences were put aside was that evening of November 11. In the face of adversity and threats against our friends' lives, we came together to support one another. No one was worried that being in that space would create drama nor were they worried that people would stare at them as if they didn't belong. We welcomed and comforted each other with open arms.

In regards to the GroupMe, we later found out that Black Penn freshmen were added to that GroupMe by a student at the University of Oklahoma who had been admitted to Penn, but ultimately chose to attend the University of Oklahoma instead. He was able to get the contact information of the Black Penn freshmen through the admitted students' class of 2020 Facebook page. Don't get me wrong, Penn took the incident very seriously—they even got the FBI involved, and they were able to trace the group back to this University of Oklahoma student. The University of Oklahoma also suspended that student, and he is no longer enrolled there.

Though Penn reacted swiftly to try and remedy the situation and make black students feel safer, many of us wondered, how many more students were out there who had these same racist thoughts and were accepted to Penn, but actually chose to attend the school and are on our campus right now? Taking down one racist student is definitely a win, but how many more students like him are out there?

Reflecting on that day, there were some people who wanted to turn this tragic instance into opportunities to shine a positive light on their individual student groups as ones who "got things done" and "cared about the black community." Some student groups tried to demonize individuals for coping with the tragedy as they saw fit even if it did not align with what their group was doing. Overall, though, it was the greatest instance of unity anyone has ever seen within Black Penn recently. In an ideal world, Black Penn would always be able to come together with this strength on a day-to-day basis—not just in the face of danger or threat. We unfortunately have not reached that day yet. However, I know that if anything like the GroupMe incident was to ever happen again, I have a community to rely on.

putting mental health & wellness first

"*Overcoming* your own personal stigma is not
an easy task, but believe me, *you are worth it.*"

fighting the stigma within ourselves

Originally published as a guest column in *The Daily Pennsylvanian,* February 9, 2014.

The first time I visited a CAPS (Counseling and Psychological Services) counselor, I felt an immediate wave of shame. It was the summer after sophomore year, and I finally began to acknowledge how my anxiety was unraveling my life. From the time I woke up to the time I went to sleep, I was hounded by incessant worrying and negative thoughts, which did nothing but erode my self-worth. I felt increasingly alone, isolated and unable to find the support that I desperately needed. Life began to feel empty, and I felt nothing like myself. I felt lost. Somehow the girl who had always had it together found herself in a CAPS office spilling her problems to a stranger. As my counselor told me, these issues are not uncommon and I could receive help through therapy. Yet, why did I feel so ashamed?

Through the numerous discussions these past few weeks, much focus has been given to the stigma of mental health. Particularly for those in minority communities, this is an issue with which we are all too familiar. When you live in a society that demands so much of your existence, life does not stop when you feel sad. For many of our families, especially without the information or resources, mental health is often misunderstood and thus we're forced to "suck it up."

For me personally, there was a piece of me that felt like a failure that day I left CAPS. There was no explanation except the fact that I didn't want to accept that I had gotten to the point where I "couldn't deal." As a black woman, the idea of being "strong" isn't just a stereotyped-character trait but rather an internalized mentality. I am guilty of telling people that I am doing fine, even when I know that it is thoroughly a lie. And I get it. Discussing mental health issues is awkward. It can make people uncomfortable, and no one wants to be judged as the "depressed friend." But despite all my fears, I knew I needed to reach out for help.

Fast-forward into the fall, and my anxiety had slowly snowballed into depression. I began to avoid people almost out of habit, and I struggled to accomplish even the smallest tasks. Every day I was drowning in my thoughts and had growing feelings of worthlessness and emptiness. I began to look for more long-term programs outside of CAPS and was fortunate enough to find free anxiety treatment at Drexel. Through this program, I have been able to better manage my thoughts and slowly find my way back to normalcy.

To those of you who are struggling with issues of your own, realize that your problems do not define you. You are so much more than a mental illness, and you can get better through therapy, medicine, or both. I know reaching out for help can be terrifying, but it is worth it. Speaking to a counselor was the last thing I ever expected to do. But despite what I had been socialized to believe about mental health issues, something inside me made the choice to get help. Something inside me made the choice to live.

While we can do our best as a campus to change the perceptions on mental illness, you cannot wait for someone to give you permission to do what is best for your health. Sometimes there won't be someone there to walk you to CAPS. Sometimes your friends will brush off your complaints as "just stress." But regardless of what others do, the least you can do is take the judgment off of yourself. Overcoming your own personal stigma is not an easy task, but believe me, you are worth it.

"Ultimately I made an *important decision*. I decided to believe in myself and I was *more successful* all around."

the sophomore slump

Penn was an adventure-filled journey for me. It was full of many ups and downs each year. While I celebrated during the high points, I lamented and struggled through the lows. These difficult times forced me to become more introspective and self-aware. One such circumstance was during my sophomore year. I vividly remember sitting in my friend's dorm room at the beginning of the year while we delighted in the onset of our second year in college. We rejoiced and giddily grinned. "Ladies, I think sophomore year might be our year!" announced another one of my friends. "We have so much to look forward to."

I guess we felt well seasoned with a year of college experience under our belts. We knew how to choose classes according to our personal preferences. Navigating lecture halls and parties was simple. Meal plans and livings on campus were officially optional. We gullibly assumed that since we'd undergone our first full year away from home, we could do it again effortlessly. Little did I know that I would experience the dreaded "sophomore slump" that same year. After that brief period of bliss in the early fall, I hit a wall—an immovable, domineering wall. It seemed as though everything I touched turned to dust.

It all began when I made the decision to start taking pre-med classes. My father and aunt—who never ceased to suggest that I wouldn't be as successful in life if I didn't study medicine—heavily influenced that decision. I unfortunately took their advice and enrolled in chemistry and calculus. These two classes were extremely challenging, to say the least. They forced me to study endlessly although I failed repeatedly. I sought many solutions including attending office hours, recording lectures, signing up for tutors, and more. None of these purported remedies got me to where I needed to be.

I felt overworked, confused, and dismayed. For the first time in my academic career, my grades weren't aligned with the amount of work I was doing. As a naïve freshman, I was so used to seeing automatic results. It was safe to conclude that if my grades weren't as high as they could be, then I wasn't working as hard as I needed to work. It had been so straightforward. However, sophomore year brought a new wave of complexity. Pulling all-nighters no longer meant that my professors would be pleased with my papers once the sun came up. Taking thorough notes no longer meant that I would get an A on an exam. I was given a wake up call that left me taken aback.

That was my academic dilemma and for a whole semester, I felt hopeless. The following semester, I was faced with similar challenges when I pressured myself into taking economics. Again, I had to deal with material that was entirely new to me. I thought I would be able to dig myself out of the grave I was in first semester, but I had no such luck. My grades weren't where they needed to be, and I unfortunately allowed this to shatter my mindset.

As if academic disappointment wasn't enough, I was served a side of social disengagement. I thought that to improve my grades, I needed to lock myself in my room and do nothing but study for days on end. I only associated with my roommates and several close friends. During first semester, my weekends were plagued with isolation and boredom. I rarely went out to enjoy myself. Aside from NSO and Halloween, I don't really recall partying. While my friends at other schools posted Facebook pictures of wild nights and fall highlights, I studied. I did homework, lab reports, and edited my resume. It was pure hell. When my parents would call, I had to decide between telling them the truth about my misery or sugarcoating it to assuage them. After a while, nothing felt purposeful or enjoyable.

Trying to be involved in student groups also felt like a chore. I was often out of the loop and struggling to juggle board member meetings with completing class readings. There were many points at which I considered resigning from all my positions to devote even more time to studying. Going to events was fun and enriching, but time consuming, nonetheless. What made my minimal extracurricular involvement even more difficult to bear was watching other sophomores balance their social and academic lives with finesse. Board presidents and chairpersons who would often brag about their course loads surrounded me. "I'm taking 5.5 credits this semester to be done with X set of requirements." "I'm taking this class now because Y professor is really engaging." "I'm going to intern with Z firm to get some early work experience." It was awful. With every borderline elitist comment, I felt more out of place, inadequate, and feeble.

Because I felt so out of touch and powerless, I began trying to control certain things that I was previously less concerned with. One of these things was my weight. In an effort to be really disciplined about my work habits, I ended up practically punishing myself with food deprivation. I would often skip meals to spend more time in front of my computer. Although I read articles about managing stress by occasionally treating oneself, I completely abandoned my favorite foods. I thought that being a workaholic meant that my mind needed to be semi-robotic. I ate the same three things every day for a couple of weeks. After this, I became used to eating so little that I began forgetting to eat at all. When I did eat, I would grab a bagful of trail mix and snack on it throughout the day. To gain even more discipline, I started abusing the gym. I went to Pottruck at least three times a week at late hours. Friends noticed that I was losing weight and commented on it. Foolishly, I started thinking of this as an upside. Even though I was losing my grip on so many other things, at least I was still in direct control of my physical appearance.

Twenty-seven pounds or more later, I realized I was being way too hard on myself. I was rapidly losing weight, but I wasn't gaining enthusiasm. I was truly selling myself short. In addition to this, I began giving up on my dreams. I once dreamt of spending a semester in France, but changed my mind because I couldn't earn pre-med credits abroad. Although I slaved through my French courses, I resisted what would have been a fulfilling reward. I also missed out on taking many intriguing classes in history, which was my favorite subject. I excluded myself from things that genuinely interested me because they didn't fit my long-term plans.

Through doing some deep reflection towards the end of the school year, I chose to switch gears. I changed my course load for the next semester. I only took courses I was fully engaged in, and that I would go on to succeed in. I renounced the need to be obsessed with classwork. I was hired to intern downtown at the district attorney's office, which was a great learning experience. I became better at balancing class with extracurricular activities. For the first time in a year, I felt like I had a social life. Ultimately I made an important decision. I decided to believe in myself and I was more successful all around. I refused to ever let myself get so dejected again.

life
after penn

"Life goes through many phases and cycles for all of us—sometimes the stressors lead to *inflammation* in our lives—but we have to find that *soothing balm of relief*, that zone of stillness in each of us, and protect it."

the itch

I am constantly fidgeting, mostly because I'm always itchy.

My skin. It's always been sensitive, prone to acne and inflammation, with itchy, dry patches in random areas like behind my ears, on the side of my neck, or underneath a breast. Once I discover that patch, I can't let it go, and must constantly pick at it and peel bits off and scratch at the hard surface until it's either removed and the soft flesh underneath is revealed or until it bleeds—either way, the skin typically grows back harder and sturdier than before, leading to a manic cycle of itching and scratching.

My hair. The texture feels coarse and uneven beneath my fingertips, shorter and longer in certain places, causing patch-like thick and thin areas that make me want to tug and pull and resize so that it's all one length. But often, the constant picking and tugging—a mindless activity while I'm thinking or working—leaves me with pieces of hair left in my hands.

My scalp. Throughout the day—many times per hour even—I scrape sections of my scalp with my fingernails and watch thick, wide, dense flakes of skin fall onto my computer keyboard, my shirt, my arm, or the notebook in front of me. I watch with a mix of glee and disgust as the flakes fall. Each flake is typically white in color, sometimes tan or shades darker, closer to my brown skin tone. Sometimes, the stubborn flakes are too densely compacted on my scalp, so I'll have to pick at it with concentration until a bit begins to peel off, oftentimes coming up with a hue of red or dark brown, meaning I've broken skin or scratched a bloody scab from my scalp. Many times, I scratch out of habit and boredom. Occasionally, I scratch because it's actually itchy.

When my three-year-old niece was born, her scalp was covered in white, dandruff-like flakes that weren't easily removed. "Cradle cap," my sister-in-law said.

"Oh no," I told her nervously, my eyes widening. "Her aunty has the adult version of this." Naturally, we shared some of the same genes. Could this condition be hereditary? I feared.

My mother told me that I was born with a white layer of skin, not unlike what appears on my scalp regularly today if I don't manage and medicate by gently lubricating the dense flakes to soften them, then gently scraping them off of my scalp with a soft, pliable silicone comb to clear the area, and finally, sealing the skin beneath the flakes with a mixture of oils, including a healing, anti-fungal tea tree oil to minimize the impact of another breakout. Never to prevent or cure—because there will always be another breakout.

I've been to dermatologists and allergists, and unfortunately, there are no cures for the eczema and seborrheic dermatitis that I have been told that I have; still, there are steroid creams and eating habits that can help me minimize the effects and make these conditions a bit more manageable. But the constant itching hasn't waned, and it has become a part of who I am. I'll never forget playing a game of charades as a kid when my younger brother acted out someone who was walking around scratching his or her head incessantly. I bent my own head down in shame as I realized that his imitation was meant to be of me. As he laughed, I felt my underarms get prickly from embarrassment; they then began to moisten and itch, but I dared not scratch anything ever again in front of him. Unfortunately, itching had already become part of my identity.

Lately, my constant physical fidgeting has manifested into mental fidgeting: anxious thoughts, overthinking, and imagining horrifying events with vivid, graphic visuals, from loved ones dying in car crashes to me screaming out horribly embarrassing statements during work meetings to me watching the reaction of others from above at my own future funeral. The visuals I seem to capture and make up in my mind feel just as intense as real life events that have actually happened. I replay conversations I had at work and think, was I too passive? Did I defend our team's work enough? I should have used this argument instead. Or maybe I was too forceful. She probably sees me as an aggressive black woman. And the cycle goes on and on.

I replay big events in my life that I planned, that meant a lot to me, like my own wedding. I should have stuck to my guns and shouldn't have ceded control over something so important to me. Why did I do that? I should have shortened the pre-wedding ceremony, or just cut it like my husband wanted; I was just so worried about my in-laws liking me or blaming me for not incorporating any of their customs. Then my mind will transport me back to that time, and I'll get my shot at a redo. I will have stood up to that in-law more confidently, more articulately, more firmly—and have even ended it with a charismatic joke as the cherry on top of getting my own way and defending myself, and that in-law will love and respect me more than ever. But then reality settles back in, and I realize that I'm in the present day, still sitting here with those regrets.

It's a never-ending game of ping pong in my head, with my mind going back and forth rethinking and regretting over and over and back again. It becomes paralyzing—I can't trust myself to make decisions because I am constantly in a state of regret about past decisions that I've made. But I can't trust others to make decisions for me because I'll regret being too passive and letting others take over for me. I try to sit with myself and understand why I cannot settle my mind, why it's becoming like an itch that I can't stop picking at—especially when the anxious feeling is the result of a great opportunity or a seemingly positive life event.

I remember taking a vacation with a group of my girlfriends. The trip came at a time when I was incredibly stressed with work. I'd just gotten put on a huge, but very ambiguous project that I was leading, and was responsible for the success of it. It was my first time working on—let alone leading—anything like it. While the timing was great because I was excited to relieve some stress by catching up with friends and relaxing in the sun on the beach, being off from work that particular week meant that I would be absent from this project that I was leading, and days would go by without me or anyone making sense of the ambiguous elements that needed resolving. Of course, I have the right to—and frankly, deserve to—take time off, but at the time I'd been feeling extremely insecure about my ability to succeed in my role at work. I feared that I might even lose my job because of my unique role that allows me to work outside of our main headquarters and return a few times per quarter. Colleagues had already made comments about it ("How'd you swing that?" or "I bet she doesn't do anything while she's away"), and I was incredibly nervous. I internalized each and every comment and would replay them in my mind as often as I would pick at my skin. So, I made the decision to take two important work calls while on vacation and allow myself to enjoy the rest of the time off.

It wasn't that I didn't feel like any other colleague could do it—I'm sure anyone else would have been great. I just felt if I was absent, there might be some confusion, since it was all so last minute, and I hadn't briefed anyone with the context needed to support the call. Sure, they might have figured it out, but it would just be better if I was there, in case they had to go to my boss or something. So, I took the calls and felt I'd found the right balance for myself on that trip. However, one friend in particular kept making comments to me each day about "always working" and the fact that she was able to "find balance" in her life and hadn't even brought her work phone with her. "I don't give in to the Man," she would say. I thought that was great—I simply wasn't in that position, at least not in that moment. (We were in completely different roles and totally different companies.) But I was happy for her to be able to do it. Unfortunately, her constant comments really got to me, and tears began to pour out of my eyes. I hated that I had to do some work during the trip, but I really didn't want to fail. I didn't want to let my friends down, but I didn't want to get a negative performance review on this project that might ultimately lead to losing my job. I got the sense that my friend thought I was so self-important that I had to take calls on vacation. The truth was that I was such a workaholic because I was not confident in my job performance and felt extremely insecure about my role. The anxiety—the mental fidgeting—had taken over; it was another vulnerable itch that I couldn't seem to soothe.

Still, beyond that moment, I do consider myself to be generally happy, a successful professional in my field of choice, with challenging, interesting projects and the trust of executives I work with that I am capable of taking on lots of projects. I feel too much pressure, but those around me say, "It's a great thing! I only wish my boss gave me more independent projects to take on and trusted me more with the most pressing initiatives at the company." It's true that it's great, but the stress and seemingly high stakes are constantly making me question my worth, whether I'm good enough and performing at a high enough caliber to warrant such trust.

I've complained to friends about the stresses of wedding planning, and the angst and confusion around so many voices in my head—between in-laws and family members and lots of competing priorities that I'm striving to balance. "At least you have a wedding to plan," they tell me. It's true—and with those words, my thoughts are diminished, deemed unworthy compared to the plight of others. Diminished in the minds of others, but still very active in my own mind.

There's a nasty truth about my anxious thinking. Despite my feelings of constant angst, I've had some truly momentous events in life. As I look back and reflect on my happiest, saddest, most frustrating, and anxiety-inducing moments, I've dealt with some tough challenges earlier in my life (about a decade ago in the years following my graduation from college), but the last three to five years have been filled with occasions that appear to be joyous on the surface or even at the start, but that have evolved into unexpectedly heartbreaking experiences. But it's something that's incredibly difficult to explain to anyone who is dealing with a deep void in their own life, something that they yearn for that perhaps you already have, whether it's a career you enjoy or a caring partner you love. It becomes a never-ending cycle of feeling hurt or sad about a difficult situation that I'm in, confiding in who I think might be a trusted friend, only to have that friend tell me that at least I have the honor of feeling that way. "At least you have a wedding to plan," I replayed in my head as I stressed about the impact of certain decisions on the lifelong relationship with my future in-laws. And then, the guilt settles in—sure, I'm stressed, but my friend is right: it is a privilege to even have this type of stress in my life. It's an ongoing cycle of stress, seeking comfort, and feeling intense guilt, which subsequently leads to even more stress. The stress makes me feel incessant angst that resurfaces my mental itching, leading me to replay and repeat the cycle.

"So how did you do it?"

"How did I do what?"

"You know—get married? Your life is so perfect."

I stifled a groan, shook my head gently, and tried to ignore the prickly, itchy feeling making its way into my armpits from within, followed by the nervous sweat beginning to form and drip down my armpits and soak into my shirt. "It's really not," I started. I began to reflect on why I was always getting these questions, why despite societal growth, there was still so much obsession about getting married. And then I began to feel guilty. People seem to think that my life is together, that my career is perfect and my marriage is perfect, only because I may appear to be happy and stress-free. I've explored why I seem to carry that perception and have worked to explain myself in an honest way when people ask how I'm doing. But at times, when I'm negative (read: honest) about frustrations happening in my life, some people trivialize them and compare them to what should be considered a greater plight that they're experiencing.

People on the outside looking in assumed that I'm "living my best life," but the stressors of even some of life's happiest, biggest changes can be anxiety-inducing and exhausting.

Even as I look ahead to potential future life events, my fear that the angsty behaviors I have developed over the years will get passed along to my future children weighs on me. Just as I feared my niece's cradle cap must have been genetic, might my mental itchiness also be hereditary?

"I'm happy for you, but I'm also sad that you made it and I didn't." I'll never forget the words that one of my dearest friends told me after I was engaged. Years later, I still hear that voice and feel horrible that she remained in a difficult situation, but also that she looked at me with that lens. What my therapist is helping me to understand today is that unfortunately, not everyone is in a place to be happy and kind to you, or to give you the type of support that you might need in a given moment. And while that's okay, it doesn't mean that friendships have to continue to live on in the same ways they have historically. This person was a great friend to me for many years, but unfortunately, we aren't able to offer each other the same comforts and level of support that we once did. It's a harsh and sad reality, and doesn't mean that we must alienate each other, but it means that we can still love and appreciate each other from afar, a bit more removed from each other's day-to-day worlds. That distance, at this time, feels healthier.

Because the truth is, some days are freaking fantastic. I do like my job, and I am happy in my marriage, I love my family, and I do feel blessed. Every week, every day is full of different feelings and ups and downs, but somewhere deep inside of me, beyond the day-to-day stressors and anxious thoughts, is a contentment, a feeling that I am on a path for me, that I can make it, that I have a community around me, that I am part of a community that supports others, that I am skilled, and talented, and happy. When I find that still place—through reading, writing, running, hiking, meditating—that contentment is there, and I have to work very hard to keep it with me more consistently. And I must remind myself that I am content—and even in the midst of feeling guilt about others, it's okay to be happy. Life goes through many phases and cycles for all of us—sometimes the stressors lead to inflammation in our lives—but we have to find that soothing balm of relief, that zone of stillness in each of us, and protect it.

for the love of you

"So I waited. And I'm *happy I waited.*"

waiting

Sex. Something every college student knows about. Something that high schoolers know about. My experience with sex is to be honest, quite negligible. I am not a sexual fiend, and it was difficult to go to Penn at times when all around me, sex was rampant. People were making out on the daily, there were condoms everywhere, and stories of people hooking up. It was an endless cycle.

That definitely wasn't my cycle. I wanted to have sex (even craved it at times, I won't lie), but I know I didn't want to have sex with the guys who came up to me, who wanted to talk to me, or who gave me their numbers. They *only* wanted sex. And while I did want sex, I didn't want to have sex and lose everything else. I didn't want to lose myself.

So I waited. And I waited. The guys at Penn were great to be friends with, but I would never date them. They were terrible to women, and I was not under the false impression that I would be the one to change them. Because that only happens in stories and this is life, this is truth.

So I waited. And I'm happy I waited.

"Give yourself the time, in mind and body, to work through
your feelings, and *don't be afraid* to act on
the therapeutic, but perhaps unnerving impulses that will
help you along the way."

time

*Dear Mark**

I have neglected to contact you since September, because I have let fear and your unpredictable behavior dictate how I handled this situation. I will not go another day without addressing you, because just as this is something I have to live with, so do you.*

You didn't ask me if I wanted to have sex. You didn't ask me if it was ok not to wear a condom. You didn't check to see if I was comfortable. You weren't worried about me at all.

The answers to the questions you should have asked—I did not want to have sex with you, in fact up until that day I had been celibate for almost a year. I would never be comfortable having unprotected sex with a strange guy that I barely knew, let alone someone that I cared about. And I wasn't comfortable. In fact I was uncomfortable, embarrassed, fearful, and completely shocked by everything that happened, and how fast it happened. Before that night you had seemed like a great guy that I could potentially trust, and within twenty minutes your whole character changed.

That night I sobbed the whole way back to my dorm and spent the night consulting my friends to figure out what the best steps were to deal with how violated and uncomfortable I felt. The following day, while you probably had a typical Wednesday, I had one of the longest and most painful days of my life: getting tested, having to take pills and painful shots. Thursday morning, I had to tell my mother and father, who didn't even know the details of my first kiss that I felt I had been violated and sexually assaulted. I missed several classes and assignments. I say all this and yet nothing I can write will fully make you understand just how much that night has affected my life.

Despite all of this, I still decided the best way to handle the situation was not formal action, but to speak with you. Though the last thing I wanted to do was have a respectful conversation, I reached out as amicably as possible. Instead of respecting my wishes your actions showed me that, again, you have no regard for anyone but yourself, you do not take no for an answer, and even if it means making me completely uncomfortable, you were going to try and force the conversation to happen when you wanted it to. At the time I thought it best not to confront you because your behavior was too sporadic and I didn't feel emotionally stable enough to speak to you in person. Even though you knew something was wrong, you made no effort to reconcile the situation following that day. You may be ok with disregarding my feelings, but I will not be able to fully move on until I know that you understand the gravity of the situation.

In closing, this was not meant to illicit a response because frankly, I don't care what you have to say or how you feel. I have never, ever had a guy treat me with as little respect or disregard as you showed me that night, and if I ever hear that you were/are involved in a similar situation, I will not hesitate to act formally.

***

I had a friend drop the letter off at his door with one of his roommates. As I waited for her to return at the end of the block, I felt the first small sense of peace I had felt in weeks. I did not fool myself into thinking it would "cure" me of the wave of emotions that I worked through almost every hour of every day following that night in September*—disbelief that I had been sexually assaulted, sadness, embarrassment, devastation, anger— but it did provide me with some much-needed fortitude. I was working through my feelings, I did what I knew it would take to help me move forward, and I had confronted my assaulter. I could get through this.

For almost a week after the incident, I felt nothing. I was numb; I felt empty. After the first week, my feelings surfaced by way of the emotional rollercoaster I described above, that would go on for months. When I couldn't hide away on Spruce or Walnut, I practically ran—eyes to the ground—down Locust Walk. I was afraid to look at any black man because I knew he had heard some altered version of the truth, afraid that others in the black community would see me only as the girl who had been sexually assaulted, or worse, just sweep my experience under the rug (as we often tend to do with topics we as a community have not learned to deal with head-on). I was terrified that I might run into my assaulter at the most inopportune time and be forced to interact. The only emotion to overcome my fear was anger that would devolve into hate. I had thrown around the word "hate" all the time before that night, we all do, but the truth of the matter was that I didn't really know what it meant to hate someone until after I was sexually assaulted. It is all consuming. How could my life be so turned around when my assaulter seemed to be thriving with an active social life within and outside Black Penn, academic success, and a list of girls he could choose from on any given weekend? As a senior, I was already feeling the pressure of figuring out the next steps, juggling six classes, and making the most out of my last few months as an undergraduate. As a black woman integrated into the black community, I was trying to navigate the near disdain I felt for some of the black men on campus after being privy to four years of relations that showcased their little regard for the treatment of women; now I had to carry around the weight of my assault and unpack all the consuming thoughts and regressive actions it impelled?

It is a testament to the support I had in the days and months following that night that I was able to work through many of those feelings, and over time, begin to heal. The best advice I received from friends just hours after the incident happened: go to Penn Women's Center. I was despondent when I arrived; I was scared, I was alone, and I didn't even know if I was in the right place. The staff immediately cleared the schedule of the Violence Prevention Educator. It was of additional comfort to know she was a black woman and an alumna. Over the next two hours, she listened to my story, comforted me, fed me my first meal since the night before, advised me on what to do to protect my sexual health, and explained to me what my rights were if I chose to take action. What I appreciated most is that she left the decision up to me.

She helped me schedule an appointment at Student Health Services within the hour; as soon as I arrived they swiftly, yet thoroughly, took me through all the necessary procedures. They were gentle, comforting, and made the experience as painless as possible, literally and figuratively.

When I decided I wanted to informally report him, getting my formal statement and "the evidence" on record in case I chose to press charges at a later date, I was assigned a Penn Police Department special detective, a black woman at my request. She transported me to the hospital on the other side of the city and stayed with me as I gave my account of the night and was administered a rape kit. Though I seemed to be interrupting my examiner's happy hour plans, or so I overheard, the detective was by my side to take me back to my dorm as soon as the process was complete. In the days that followed, she checked in periodically to make sure I was doing ok.

To those women affiliated with the University I encountered that day, I thank you—in my fragile state I am so grateful to have been in your trustworthy and empowering hands.

From there it was time. The support of friends. Instead of avoiding my emotions, which would boil over with great resurgence anyway, I began to deal with them and accept my reality—my feelings wouldn't just go away. I was able to get a few appointments at CAPS throughout the last two semesters, though nowhere near the frequency I would have liked. At my request the special detective notified my teachers of extenuating circumstances and they were very accommodating in the weeks to follow with assignments and missed classes. I even felt whole enough to attend Take Back the Night in the spring and share a piece of my story, which proved to be a very therapeutic experience.

There was only one resource I felt I lacked throughout my experience; I didn't really know any other undergrads or recent grads who could relate to what I went through and in the same context, as someone dealing with sexual assault within the black community. I hope my story can serve as that relatable piece for someone else that has had, or will have, the tremendous misfortune to go through a similar experience. You are not alone. Please consider the resources and options available to you, and as the University continues to address how sexual assault is defined and treated, as well as mental health, hopefully the list of resources is ever growing. Give yourself the time, in mind and body, to work through your feelings, and don't be afraid to act on the therapeutic, but perhaps unnerving impulses that will help you along the way.

And lastly, to the black women who have spoken out about their sexual assault experiences following my graduation, and are working to ensure every sexual assault victim gets the necessary support they need on campus: I salute you, and I thank you for your courage.

*Name and dates have been changed.

"I have now *learned* this: I am a *woman* and I am *not safe* in this world."

a letter to my sisters about our brothers

I know that having discussions with men about feminism proves difficult because I am forever apologizing. I find myself apologizing to these men, my friends, for the actions of other men, in order to exonerate them from what the majority have done. Of course, I wish to draw a line of demarcation, documenting the ways in which patriarchal systems of oppression are only caused by "those" boys over there. But as all mathematical equations go, they too are variables of ignorance, inaction, or participation. I cannot leave them out.

This evening I talked to a good friend about the dangers of party culture. I described to him my biggest fear: that many men our age, older and younger, dwell in dual realities, where jerking a girl against a wall is acceptable on a Saturday night and respectability politics apply every other day of the week. I call this dangerous intentionally. It endangers you and me, black millennial women, for the same reason it impairs men emotionally, socially, and intellectually. We are not safe with our brothers. It is not enough for me to sit idly by and just "not go to the party." Whether or not this truth is edible, what one man is capable of doing in the dark, he will assuredly find a cousin of action for in the light, in the classroom, in my dorm, in a cafeteria, an office space, at the highest level of the court.

It is impossible to treat a woman one way and not believe she is worthy of that same treatment in another context. It is impossible to have the capacity to grab, twist, jerk, dagger, push, slap, bend over, and curse at a woman then to believe she is anything but deserving of such actions in each and every other context in which she is encountered. The disregard for women's humanity is all but becoming for our friends, our brothers, our fathers, our lovers. And it impairs them from truly being able to recognize these wrongs whilst they continue to prove and perform their masculinity.

My friend doesn't believe these acts are acts of violence. Instead he calls them disrespectful. Violence, he believes, is reserved for anything that physically hurts you. To be honest, I thought pain was subjective. I know this goes back to the performance. The words we use cancel or heighten our realities of these situations, these "womanly" oppressions. But this again is the danger. Because if these small acts are refused to be seen as acts of violence, which by definition is the unlawful exercise of physical force or intimidation, then neither will the continuation of them (which is defined as assault, battery, molestation, rape).

I speak from a context colored in a history of the diaspora when I say black men must join this conversation. Together, we must unpack the aversion to seeing acts of violence, however brief, as what they are: unsafe, unjust, deeply damaging, and irrevocably wrong. I grew up and was taught to be an obedient woman. A careful woman. A neatly dressed, don't look him in the eye, stay quiet and don't walk at night, hold a key in between your fingers on the walk home, tell him you have a boyfriend, kind of woman. But my brothers simply grew. At best were told to wear belts and take out the trash on Thursdays.

I have now learned this: I am a woman and I am not safe in this world. Every day this summer on my way home, I've had to run. Perhaps it is a privilege to walk and not be stalked by men, idle on a corner. Every day this summer I have passed men who believed my body was a place waiting to marry their dirty thoughts, their masturbatory misogyny. It was once my childhood privilege to have believed my body belonged deeply to myself. That it wasn't a whiteboard waiting to be filled with the hateful and ugly commentary of men. And every day this summer, I have thanked God that this time, I made it home without being called a bitch. Without being grabbed. Or chased. Or cornered. Or raped. Or killed.

Every day I woke up and I came home and said the same prayer: thank God for today, because you survived.

And I still say it for myself. I say it for my mother, my aunt, my sister, my cousins, I say it for my best friends. I say it for every single woman on the street in every corner of the world who walks in the forsaken light and flesh of female.

As of today, I will not apologize for these truths to our brothers:

You think feminism is a dirty word. That I don't need it, that it's attacking you, that it belongs in the mouth of a thing and not a person, of a woman and therefore, not an equal. But tell me, brother, how it feels to exist in an anatomy and fear for your life every single day?

"In all, she was *beautiful*, and he wondered why she didn't
have a boyfriend yet.

'I dunno,' she gazed into the distance, '*You tell me*.'"

through smoke

This fictional story is based on a real experience.

He didn't expect to find her there.

There was a pair of benches outside of their dorm right in between their residence and another, settled between a few small trees. Students only sat on those benches to have private phone conversations that weren't private enough for their rooms, or used it as a place of rest after stocking up at the nearby supermarket.

She sat on the far right bench, balancing a cigarette between her lips. Deftly, almost like a reflex, her lighter was aflame and the end was lit. He didn't know she smoked.

They locked eyes as soon as she inhaled. From where he stood he could only see the floating red dot her cigarette made in the dusk, but he could tell she regarded him for a while. As she exhaled the first round of smoke, he made his way over.

"Hey!" he waved.

She didn't reply but moved her backpack from the space beside her. He took the seat. "Finally done with midterms," he sighed. "This week was too stressful."

"Mmm," she replied, inhaling slowly.

He regarded her from where he sat. In the light of the pink sun he saw her long neck craning slightly forward, her cheekbones high like a model's. Her brown eyes caught the light and glistened with pieces of gold. She recently shaved her head, no hair to speak of, so her profile was clean and sleek. Smoke streamed from her lips and formed wispy ribbons about her face, a perfect scene for a black and white photo.

In all, she was beautiful, and he wondered why she didn't have a boyfriend yet.

"I dunno," she gazed into the distance, "You tell me." The smoke seemed to form each word as she spoke.

A little embarrassed he looked away for a moment. Freudian slip.

"But I already told you why," he smirked as he looked back at her.

After saying this he could see her eyes shift slowly in his direction. He smiled and nodded slightly as if to say, "You know what I'm talking about." Her eyes remained fixed on him, unblinking.

"When?" she asked.

"When I texted you the other day," he said, still smiling. "Remember?"

"Oh." Her gaze shifted forward again, her eyes looking at nothing in particular. She took a small drag from her cigarette, held it in for a moment, then let two streams of smoke jet from her nose. "Yeah. That."

He didn't know her to be this quiet. Normally she was loud, energetic and, to put it simply, weird. "But in a good way," he always said to her, and he meant it. Talking to her was a different experience every time, her eyes lighting up as she spoke. She could carry on a conversation about something as random as sea urchins (he didn't put it past her), and he always found himself thoroughly entertained. Now the only light he could see was the glittering gold of the setting sun settling on the lower half of her eyes.

"Yep," he looked in the direction she was looking, "You kinda talk a lot. Only do that when a guy is with you."

He could see her slowly shake the ash from the end of the cigarette, and he could tell that she didn't like his piece of advice. He knew he was right, though.

"Tell me something," she inhaled once more, slowly and deliberately. "Am I talking a lot now?"

He kept his gaze ahead of him and let out a sigh. "No…but you normally do."

"Mhm." She tilted her head back and blew a smoke ring.

"Is there something wrong?" he asked. He had sensed a growing tension ever since he sat down.

"I'll let you think about that," she replied and blew another, slightly smaller smoke ring.

He sighed once more and leaned forward on the bench. She was acting differently than usual, which in her case was weird. Talking to her turned into a chore, and all he wanted was a nice conversation, maybe even mess with her a bit. And he didn't have that much time to spend with her, anyway. He had other things to do.

"Well if you're not in the mood to talk," he got up from the bench, "I will see you later."

Just as he said this he heard his phone trill.

She looked at him as he took his phone out of his pocket.

"What?" he asked.

"She's coming over, isn't she?" She threw what was left of her cigarette on the ground and crushed it with her foot.

"She's my girlfriend," he said as he texted a reply, "so yes."

She leaned forward on the bench and rested her hands on her lap. "You really love her, don't you?"

He sent the message and hoisted his bag over his shoulder. "More than anything."

He started walking to the dorm when she called out, "Then who am I to you?"

He paused. Without looking back he asked, "Why are you asking me that?"

"Because I want to know where I fit in your life."

Turning his head, he saw the gold glittering fiercely in her eyes. Her expression never changed during the whole conversation, but he got it as one line of gold made its way down her face.

"Please don't…not now."

"I'm sorry," another line of gold slid down her face, "but we really need to talk."

"No, we don't."

"Yes, we do."

"My girlfriend just texted me and she's meeting me in my room in like, ten minutes."

"Ten minutes is enough time."

"No, it's *not*, and I really don't feel like doing this with you."

"Doing what with me?" she sneered. "Anything other than fucking me?"

At this he dropped his bag and turned around. He made his way over to her and met his face with hers.

"What the hell is that supposed to mean?" he glared.

She stood up and met his gaze. "You know exactly what I mean."

"What is your freaking *problem* today?!"

"The only freaking *problem* I have is you treating me like I don't matter."

"You matter!"

"Yeah, only when you're horny and she's gone for the night."

"*Seriously*? Is that really how you think I feel about you?"

"Oh!" she said, putting her hands to the sides of her head in fake astonishment. "I'm sorry. I forgot you get horny during the daytime, too."

"You mean more to me than that…"

"Then you have a *great* way of proving it."

"No, I prove myself just fine. I'm just not proving myself in the way that you want."

At this a few more lines of gold cut black streaks down her cheeks. Her lower lip began to quiver as she broke her gaze and looked away from him. "What makes her so special…" she whispered.

"Everything." He sighed. He didn't like that she was here crying in front of him, that her heart was breaking and he couldn't give her what she wanted. But what was he supposed to do? He liked her a lot, but he loved his girlfriend. He couldn't just leave her for someone else.

She looked back at him, her eyes stinging from the salty mascara mixture that was forming. She wiped it away with her hand, then frowned as she looked at the mascara that smeared her skin. She let out a sigh. Through his glasses he looked back at her, feeling safe behind the glass that separated the pain in her eyes from the guilt in his.

"Apparently 'everything' doesn't include sex, right?" she finally asked as she pulled out a pack of cigarettes from her jacket pocket.

"Yeah, it's frustrating," he looked at the ground, trying to avoid looking at her, "but that's the price I pay for falling in love."

"To be honest," she said as she pulled a new cigarette from the pack, "that price was cheap."

Her words hit him like a speeding truck that jack-knifed into his chest, leaving him speechless. He looked back at her and saw that the cold expression she had worn before had returned. Her eyes, which had a sort of intensity to them earlier, were dim. She didn't look at him, but instead got her bag and hoisted it onto her back as she stood up. She brushed off her jeans, adjusted her jacket, and put the cigarette between her lips.

"Well I guess I have my answer," she said to herself. She took her lighter from her pocket, flicked on a flame, and lit the end.

She inhaled, then let two streams of grey smoke jet from her nose. All these motions she did without looking at him, like he was invisible to her. Without a goodbye or even a side-glance, she started walking in the opposite direction of their dorm, a cloud of smoke trailing behind her. As she walked away, she hummed a tune to herself, the click of her heels keeping the beat. He only knew her to do something like that.

As he saw her walk away, his phone began to vibrate and trill again, but this time it didn't stop. His girlfriend was calling, probably to ask him where he was.

He pulled out his phone from his pocket, stared at the screen, then quietly hit "decline."

"The more we *experience* in life, the more we learn
about ourselves, and it's this constant *redefinition*
of *self-love and understanding* that allows us to grow."

love you

This love story starts how most of the great ones do: Boy meets girl. Boy likes girl. Boy courts girl. Boy wins girl. Boy loves girl. Boy dumps girl. Girl is devastated and spends the summer chugging wine like it's nobody's business…wait, *pause*.

So maybe I lied a little bit—this love story is definitely not like most. **SPOILER ALERT**: They don't live happily ever after; however, there is a happy ending. It's so funny how things don't always end up the way we expect them to…but I digress. Let me rewind a little bit.

I met my ex-boyfriend, or "Mr. Man" as I'll call him, when I was about fifteen years old. I can't remember exactly how I met him, but in a city like St. Louis with an average two degrees of separation instead of six, you tend to cast a wide net as far as your social circle is concerned. Though we didn't attend the same schools, he somehow managed to always be in the mix. I never thought too much of him outside of our casual friendship. He was definitely a nice guy, but being anything more than friends simply never crossed my mind. We virtually lost touch after high school, but he resurfaced around my junior year of college; one of my best friends had reconnected with him, and through her he expressed a lingering interest in me. Naturally, I was flattered. You see, as the girl who always struggled with self-confidence, I had come to believe that when a guy said you were cute, you weren't supposed to think twice. "Just go for it!" had become my motto. However, I had yet to fully experience the repercussions of that rather fucked up perspective.

Allow me to explain.

Do you remember those annual trips to the doctor's office your parents dragged you to as a kid? It was always the same routine: they measured your height, recorded your weight, tested your reflexes, etc. At the end of your visit, however, the doctor always brought out a certain special chart. This lovely chart, commonly known as the height-to-weight ratio chart, was a favorite of my doctor's. I, however, *despised* that damn chart.

It served as my yearly reminder that I was in the ninety-ninth percentile for both my height and my weight...and I was still growing. As a black kid in a predominately white environment, I already stuck out like a sore thumb, but this chart only further confirmed that I would never look like my other classmates. Damn, that chart was the WORST.

In hindsight, what I should have done was strut my tall, chunky self out of my doctor's office and said, *"You don't know me! You don't know my life!"* Unfortunately, I wasn't that headstrong as a child, and I instead allowed moments like these to chip away at my self-confidence. I hit a point during my adolescence where I couldn't even look at myself in the mirror because I mercilessly picked at and criticized every part of my body. Once I got to high school, however, I learned that such intense self-deprecation was far from "cute," and even my closest friends were starting to get annoyed with how much I put myself down. Hence, I developed a "fake it 'til you make it" mentality to get me through my days. I made a conscious effort to mask my dissatisfaction with my physical appearance by drawing the attention elsewhere; I focused on excelling academically, socially, athletically, etc. Over time, this turned out to be a pretty solid strategy, as I finally felt like I had something to be proud of. Before too long, my artificial sense of confidence was fairly convincing...so much so that I actually started believing it was real. I found myself genuinely embracing my accomplishments, and being less of a tough critic. I was working towards genuinely being happy with myself by embracing what I couldn't change and celebrating what made me beautiful. Where I wasn't as convincing, however, was in my interactions with the opposite sex. Deep down I couldn't seem to shake that big-little-kid mentality, fearful of that stupid chart and so rattled by the fact that I would never look like the average girl. As such, I wasn't the most selective when it came to welcoming male attention—that's not to say I didn't have any standards (let's not get crazy now), I just wasn't always as meticulous in my selection.

Fast-forward to my junior year, where in the blink of an eye my once casual friendship with Mr. Man quickly turned into something much heavier than your average relationship. His interest sparked a mutual attraction, and things escalated from there. We spent an entire semester figuring out exactly how to make "us" work, and the next full year fostering, and then destroying, what will forever be my first love.

Prior to being with Mr. Man, I had heard that falling in love was like being on an unimaginable high. You get so wrapped up in the essence of the other person that you can't fathom leaving their side. You put their needs before your own, and have more regard for "we" than "me." Essentially, you're to give yourself to the one you love, naturally expecting to be given a piece of their heart in return. This all sounded extremely corny to me, but I also found it to be surprisingly real. The love I had for Mr. Man initially felt like that unimaginable high. I threw myself into our relationship head first, fully committing to what it meant to be "his." I let myself go in a way that I never had before, and got caught up in what it felt like to love and be loved in return. It's true: Love makes you feel a little loopy, but the right type of love is supposed to leave you extremely fulfilled. Unfortunately, this was far from the right love for me.

While the most intricate details of the demise of my relationship with Mr. Man will always remain sacred, I will say this: how I handled myself in my relationship was a direct result of my wavering self-worth. I allowed my insecurities to hold me back from being honest with myself…and with him. I won't discredit the fact that our love felt real at the time, but despite the love we had for each other, we simply brought out the worst in each other. We struggled with practically everything, from physical distance to jealously and distrust. We broke up, made up, and drove each other insane more times than I would like to admit. We made a habit of avoiding tough conversations, failed to speak up when things didn't seem right, and feared eventually ending something that we both knew *needed* to end. What hurt most, however, was the notion that everything I had given to Mr. Man was for nothing. Letting him take the things I was most proud of about myself and turn them into something to be ashamed of nearly crippled me. He had a piece of me that I couldn't relinquish. Ultimately, I was so wrapped up in the idea of someone finally loving me that I ignored the signs it wasn't meant to be.

I wish I could say that I was the one to end things for good, but you remember the beginning of this story, right? Eventually, Mr. Man was the one to pull the plug on us not one month after I graduated from Wharton and returned home for the summer. I was absolutely devastated. Here I was, a recent Ivy League grad spending my last real summer hopelessly pining after the guy who broke my heart. I was terrified for the summer to end, when the time would come for me to leave for San Francisco and close my Mr. Man chapter for good. I wasn't ready, but I knew had to go. Lucky for me, it was the best thing that could have ever happened.

See, didn't I promise that this story would have a happy ending?

Through all of the trials of my relationship with Mr. Man, I learned an extremely valuable lesson: you can't expect to find love with someone else until you truly know and love yourself. And I don't mean knowing like naming your favorite color or how you like your eggs cooked in the morning, I mean *really* being in touch with the essence of who you are. At the time, I couldn't let go of Mr. Man because I was so crippled by the thought of someone who once claimed to love everything about me falling so quickly out of love with me. I put so much of my self-worth into his hands, almost completely derailing years of working hard at finding myself again. I was ashamed to admit that I had become so dependent on the thoughts and actions of someone else, yet I continued to throw myself into something I didn't truly believe in anymore. It was only when I completely removed myself from him that I started to understand why everything happened the way it did. I firmly believe that all things happen for a reason, and while we may not always be privy to the "why," we always come out with at least a little bit of appreciation for the "how."

I will forever be grateful for my relationship with Mr. Man, because in the wake of our breakup I was able to embark on a journey twenty-two years in the making. I took a step back to think holistically about who I was, what I wanted for myself, and how I was going to fall back in love with the best parts of me. Now I would be lying through my teeth if I said I was at the end of my journey, but that's not necessarily a bad thing. The more we experience in life, the more we learn about ourselves, and it's this constant redefinition of self-love and understanding that allows us to grow. The best moments along this journey, however, are those "ah-ha!" moments that help build upon your foundation and give you a stronger sense of self. In these moments, you find the confidence to be clear and unwavering in how you present yourself each and every day, and the cojones to tell someone to "fuck off" if they try to knock you off of your game.

Now twenty-four years into my journey, I'm extremely proud of the person I am today, and I definitely could not have said that two years ago. While I may not have it all figured out quite yet, I am excited for what's to come, because as the great poet Carrie Bradshaw once said, *"**the most exciting, challenging, and significant relationship of all is the one you have with yourself. And if you find someone to love the you you love, well, that's just fabulous.**"*

no regrets

"Penn was the birthplace and the *nexus of my two worlds*, where social consciousness and identity politics were nurtured and individual ambitions in a strong pre-professional environment ran deep, but *were always at war*."

pieces of me

As a million, flailing hands fought for my attention during "flyer week," I strolled down Locust Walk negotiating between the exposed bricks I needed to avoid and the right people I should listen to. I came to Penn with some preconceived notions about a few organizations based upon my older high school friends who were then sophomores. Each student group thought it was better than all the others, one person always had more intriguing catch phrases coupled with the perfect afternoon treat, and some groups could sell themselves based upon their brand name alone. With this knowledge, pacing my way through the main artery of campus became a didactic moment that set up the trajectory for how I navigated my time at Penn. I became adept at filtering out the fluff and follies, in the same manner that I selected my extracurricular activities that day on Locust. With so many niche communities, Penn has the uncanny ability to stretch people too thin and cause them to inadvertently lose sight of themselves. Over those four pivotal years, I found that I needed to be the best protector of my ego, and the most efficient measurer of my happiness. Time taught me that I am the only one who has to live my life each day and no one else has to be comfortable in it but me. I grew into a strong gatekeeper of what I belonged to and how people can impact me in my own space. Thus, one of the biggest lessons I took away from Penn was the importance of self-preservation.

Before coming to Penn, I had a very different outlook on life. My parents were both 41-year-old adults with established careers before they decided to have me. Yet, they gave me all their attention, time, resources, and affection when they were not at work. My relationship with my parents had always been there, but it wasn't always comfortable. Throughout my entire life, the power dynamic between us was very traditional and authoritative. I have always been disciplined and received praise from their contemporaries about how well-raised I was, that I carried myself with dignity and class, and that they hoped I would rub off on their kids, with whom I was friends. All of this of course stroked my parents' egos and made them proud.

Yet what holds true is that my parents have always made it their priority that I am comfortable in my own skin as long as it did not come in conflict with their images of themselves and how they were perceived by the rest of their community. I played the actor, and they were the audience. I performed, and they provided me with the things I wanted in order to play the role they saw most fit. My parents taught me that if I worked hard and maintained excellence in the classroom, I would get everything I wanted out of life. They reinforced this ideal to the best of their abilities by almost always making that possible. If I got all As in a semester, I could go on shopping sprees. Once I did better than that, I had a fabulous sweet sixteen and got my own car. If I was recognized for my leadership ability in an extracurricular activity, then I was given more freedom to go places like study abroad in Spain as a sophomore in high school and to visit friends across the country that I met through all the programs I participated in. With that said, I had a lot of control over most things that many young people yearn for, like my own means of transportation, reliable and positive friendships, and a mastery of work and play. Nevertheless, I am grateful that Penn showed me that that's not how life always works.

Surprisingly enough, in an institution rife with privilege and entitlement, I started to unlearn and unravel those previously established outlooks that my parents shrouded my eyes with. I stopped "performing" for others to a certain degree. I continued to work hard, but not as tirelessly as I did in high school. I never forgot the premonition from a middle school teacher who told me that he feared I would burn out one day. I could say that had a huge impact on how I approached my time at Penn, but that would be the easy way out. In reality, I grew disillusioned from the idea that working hard, playing by the rules, and using all the resources available to me, would always be sufficient.

The black code of "working twice as hard just to get half of what they have" has always been taxing. Perhaps it was pulling off the rose-colored lenses after finishing my urban education class? Or maybe it was the constant frustrations of seeing the myth of meritocracy come alive in areas even outside the classroom? This applied to the courses I thought I could handle (but resulted with my first Cs), each internship I worked tirelessly for and still didn't receive an offer from in return, and romantic relationships I expected to have, but didn't. Nevertheless, I've always had my Dad in the back of my head bellowing, "remember who you are" anytime I stepped out the door of our home and I think his "gentle nudge" served me well as I adapted to setbacks. Even though I did not get a "reward" for when I did the right thing or put in my all—the integral difference was that I didn't let all of these moments sully my sense of self.

At the same time, this strong self-preservation was also made possible by some of the people who positively influenced me throughout my time at Penn. Through the supportive relationships I cultivated in Sister Sister, Makuu, Penn Women's Center, and Pennacle, I engaged with people in a way that I never would have imagined. For the first time in my life, I gained male confidants who were in sync with my emotional and psychological needs. Whether it was through launching Sister Sister or playing a role in BWUA after I returned from abroad, they celebrated my strengths and pushed me to use them and contribute to the black community. Equally important, they admired my maintenance of self-respect as a woman, which was sadly hard to come by with all of the collegial temptations that exist on campus. They assured me that I would not look back on the path I chose in vain and that made me feel good. With my male friends, I felt more empowered to talk about a variety of things that bothered me in general, something that I never dealt with at home because I was always encouraged to keep things to myself and guard my heart. I grew less detached from my emotions and started to feel the inherent power of vulnerability.

It is amazing that distance from my parents made me more comfortable when making my own choices. I pushed back on them without the stress of possible retaliation because I was not under their roof. I shared more with them about what was happening at school via Skype and text, and in the spirit of reciprocity they somehow began to do the same. Whether it was the "less return on your investment" major I decided to pursue, or the time I strategically planned to get birth control before my first time, my parents were in the know and to my surprise, happy to be engaged in my life in a way they had never been before. These experiences at Penn pushed me into the driver seat, and I am proud that I was able to take them along for the ride.

As I am two years removed from college, I have seen how my initial tactics apply now more than ever. The rat race does not relent. Some people will judge you for not taking a pay cut to pursue your passion, large firms will remind you that you are just a cog in the wheel if you get too comfortable, others will continue to be overpaid for a job that they don't even deserve, and I know I am not alone when beating myself up about wanting to go back to grad school, albeit one that must be the same caliber of Penn or better. I've already encountered stumbling blocks in my job that initially made me question my intelligence and if I even belong there. Yet I remembered that I had the same support of those friends from Penn and my loving parents, so why would I let my self-concept change now?

Thankfully, I look back at it as the best example of how I strengthened my resolve to do anything I put my mind to and overcome said obstacle. Penn was the birthplace and the nexus of my two worlds, where social consciousness and identity politics were nurtured and individual ambitions in a strong pre-professional environment ran deep, but were always at war. Learning how to balance these two worlds successfully while in college was tremendously helpful because it has now contributed to my self-preservation in the real world. As a young professional woman in New York, I maintain a sense of equilibrium with my involvement in New York Needs You, mentoring ESL and first-generation college students as a career coach, and the Senator Gillibrand Mentoring Initiative, participating in a new program to boost the number of women in corporate boardrooms by tapping 100 executives from top businesses to mentor young women like myself.

The only problem is that there are no more flyer weeks. I don't have easy access to countless organizations to join or causes to support with like-minded individuals who can double as roommates and mentors in a small-square radius. There are no experts to effectively vet all of my choices for the next best job or hobby, because they don't fall neatly under one roof or network like in the good old days. To pursue my happiness now, I have to aggressively research clubs, determine time commitments or distance from work, and scour online getaway deals that meet all of my friends' price points. Essentially, I have to be active in all things that I do. Penn exposed me to what is out there in the universe, social constructs, beautiful confidants, shocking viewpoints, unspoken truths, and incredible opportunities, but now I am confident with the task to find and take what is right for me, and me only.

"Please, give me *abnormal*. Give me *absurd*. Give me *uncomfortable*. Give me *phenomenal*. Give me *film*. Give me *theatre*."

on dreams, passion, and how to succeed at penn

Summer 2013. Woke up, showered, brushed my teeth, grabbed my bag, and headed outside. Slipped into the metro doors just in time. Took a breath. Looked up and took in what was around me. Suits, business casual, designer bags, briefcases, morning coffee, and small conversation. Abrupt stop. Work from nine to five. Return home and prepare to do it all over again. That summer I realized that I didn't want this to be my life. I knew that I could never live the traditional corporate life so I finally found the courage to stop running. I had to ask myself why I would ever choose to live in this black and white world when I have the power to play in the grey area. That meant that I chose art. I chose sharing stories that matter. I chose the power of performance because I don't want to be that person; that person that gave up their dreams because they had to think practically. Please, give me abnormal. Give me absurd. Give me uncomfortable. Give me phenomenal. Give me film. Give me theatre.

The executive suite life is not for me and it has not been easy coming to terms with this fact. Being an African American girl from a low-income household, I put a lot of pressure on myself to be successful in the most practical professions. It was only in my senior year, that I redefined what success means and what my contribution to my community will be. Throughout my time at Penn, I became a passionate spectator of performance. I grew to understand that different mediums of art could change lives. It can give people hope, feed people's dreams, and serve as a reminder of reality in addition to becoming an escape from it. With every role including Beneatha in Raisin in the Sun, Elizabeth from In the Next Room, the Moaner in Vagina Monologues, or even the characters I played in the small films directed by my peers, I learned something about myself and found a greater purpose by sharing those stories with others. As I become the character, I look to connect with people so that they have an opportunity to validate experiences in their own lives and to discover something new about themselves. Acting has provided sanity and clarity in my life from the day I picked up a script. My only dream is to wake up and live my life as an actress and to indulge in whatever calmness or chaos that brings me.

My name is Kalyne Coleman, and I'm a 2014 graduate from the University of Pennsylvania with a bachelor of arts degree in communication and minor in theatre. In a couple of weeks, I will be attending the Actors Studio Drama School at Pace University in order to pursue my master of fine arts in acting. I shared this story with you all to shed light on my creative journey through college. One of my biggest life lessons at Penn was realizing that it is okay to follow your passion, whatever that might be. Despite outside pressures, being happy and attempting to use your passion to make the world a better place is all that matters. My experience in the arts community at Penn and especially in the African American Arts Alliance (4A), my second family, made me a better person and ultimately led me to realize who I am and who I see myself becoming.

Undergrad life at UPenn can be a lot of things. Confusing, exciting, frustrating, and amazing all at the same time. You are about to be challenged in ways that you have never been before. You will question things that you never have and meet people that you never thought you would. This experience will definitely teach you how to think differently. There will be smarter people, you will be pushed harder, and for the first time in your lives you get to choose for the most part what you want to study. In addition to the new academic world that you'll be entering, you are also going to learn about life. You will have a new independence and freedom and you have the opportunity to make the next four years of your life, unforgettable. With that said, I would like to share my top ten keys to success. By no means is this a guide on how to be a perfect student, but these are lessons I learned that helped me grow into the woman I am today.

1. Ask for help.

This is one of the most important lessons that you will ever learn and it needs to be engrained in you by the time you finish this article. ASK. FOR. HELP. This is the make or break for so many students! When you are struggling, put your pride aside and reach out to those who can offer you assistance. Know the resources that UPenn has available whether that be the tutoring office, a center specific to your culture (Makuu and Africana have your back), or a counseling service, and go to them. That is what they are there for. Matter fact, don't wait until you're struggling. Go before that and prevent these issues from happening.

2. Get to know the people that can help you survive in college.

- Starting with your professors and TAs (or teaching assistants). Go to office hours/get to know them. Even if you don't have questions or have a 4.0…go anyway. It makes a difference if they know who you are, trust me.
- Get to know your financial aid officer. Money is a crucial struggle in college but you'd be surprised how much people are willing to help when you put forth effort. Also, if your financial aid officer isn't working out, reach out to someone else until you find the person who works for you.
- Find a mentor who went down a similar path that you're interested in and
- NETWORK! Do your research. Get to know important people. It'll help you in the long run.
- Also, don't underestimate the power of your peers as mentors. Your friends can pretty much help you through anything.

3. HAVE FUN! But please, please, please be smart about it.

- I've always been the type of person who likes to have the best of both worlds. The person who studies but also parties. Its possible, but it's definitely a balancing act.
  There is nothing wrong with enjoying yourself however you like to have fun, but do it in doses. Please don't let the façade of partying, drinking, dating, and whatever else cloud the reason you are truly there. Just in case you forgot, you are there to learn and to set yourself up to be successful in the future!
- Additionally, please don't waste your freshman year. I can't tell you

how many of my friends wish they could go back to their freshman year and try again for a better GPA. Once it's done it's done. You can't get that time or those classes back and you will spend the rest of your college career playing catch up. Don't do it to yourself.

- Look into your classes. Find out what people are saying about the professor and the workload, and prepare yourself. Lastly, don't overwhelm yourself with too many extracurricular activities. Take a breath. Choose one or two that you love and focus on the balancing act.

4. Follow your passion, but don't pass up the opportunity to try something new.

Please don't get comfortable in your group of friends and activities and fail to take advantage of all that Penn has to offer. You don't have to do what you've always done. This is your time to try what you want and if it doesn't work out you can try something else until you find your niche. That's the beauty of college.

5. Surround yourself with like-minded groups of people.

- Surround yourself with people who are moving forward. Working hard to do their best and that want the same for you. Not everyone will have your best interests in mind so you have to be cautious when choosing your friends. Be smart and listen to your instincts. Dr. Angelou once said, "The first time someone shows you who they are believe them."
- Someone also once told me in an inspirational speech that it is so important to have friends that are better than you in some regard. It may sound crazy, but listen. If you are the smartest person in your group of friends, something is wrong. If you have the best style…the most talent…something has got to change. You have to surround yourself with people who will help you grow. People who can pull you up and make you better. Not saying that there is anything wrong with helping your friends, but you shouldn't always be the one helping. Be smart about your friend choices.

6. Figure out how you best handle stress.

Whether it is a quiet place? Music? Exercise? Prayer? Whatever. Find what works for you and do it. College is fun but it can be soooo stressful. Don't let it consume you because there's always a way out.

- Sidenote: If you are attempting to follow the motto, I'll sleep when I'm dead…#fail…Don't do that. Don't think that. I know. It will eventually catch up to you. For example, during my senior year finals I stayed up for forty-eight hours—you never want that to be you. #TheStruggle I know me saying this won't stop those late night coffees and early morning Red Bulls but hey…learn for yourself.
- On a more serious note, I want to reinforce the importance of mental health. This can be a scary and often taboo subject especially in the minority community, but please don't ignore it. If you need to talk to someone, be that a mentor or a counselor at CAPS, do it. You are worth it and you should not be ashamed of that. Unfortunately during my senior at Penn, there were a number of suicides that happened. As a reaction to this, our community is ready for a change and is open now more than ever to have this conversation and to put mental health in the forefront so that we can develop strong and healthy beings. Be a part of that change. Don't let the conversation stop and never shame someone for getting the help they may need.

7. Do things that matter.

This point speaks for itself but I will take this opportunity to share a few of the organizations/movements I was a part of. In my senior year, I was the President of the Gamma Epsilon Philadelphia City Chapter of Alpha Kappa Alpha Sorority, Incorporated, the Marketing Director/Ongoing Actress for 4A, the Co-Coordinator for the Penn Arts pre-freshman program, Social Chair for Onyx Senior Honor Society, actress in Vagina Monologues, and a mentor in the Gates Millennium Scholars Program. In my time at Penn, I was also involved in the Black Student League, Black Wharton, and the Center for Africana Studies. All of these experiences contributed to my undergrad experience and I wouldn't change my time in any of them for the world.

By the way, STUDY ABROAD. That's a thing and it matters. It will change your life. The three months I spent in London were literally the best three months of my college career. I travelled. I discovered. I lived. I loved. It was everything.

8. Being a leader does not mean being perfect.

Don't beat yourself up over mistakes. We all make them. Just learn from them and keep growing.

Remember that mistakes happen. Whether it was that missed exam, that email you wish you never sent, that party you had no business going to, that class that shall remain nameless, that thesis…that break up—that led to that make up, those all-nighters, that interview that just went wrong, that moment when you ran out of excuses. Life is about those moments because it is in those moments that we discover who we are and what we need to do to change.

9. Say thank you.

I am extremely blessed to have people around me who are constantly supporting me and making sure that I have everything I need. My parents are two people who have pushed me from the beginning and are always there and I thank them as much as I can but it's not just your family and friends that you have to remember to thank. Be sure to reach out to your teachers, administrators, and mentors who have given their time, wisdom, knowledge, and even money to make sure you made it to where you are today. I am now an African American woman graduating from an Ivy League institution without debt (shout out to all of the Gates Millennium Scholars), and I'm proud of that.

With that said, don't forget to thank yourself. For working hard, staying focused, and doing it big!

10. Don't run away from your dreams—embrace them. That's the

crazy thing about a passion: it will keep chasing you.

Once you figure out what makes you happy…what makes you smile. Don't let that go because you're afraid.

And on that note I'm done with my top ten keys to success. You all have the potential for greatness. You just have to believe that you can do it. Remember that you're a work in progress and "you must begin to think about yourself as becoming the person you want to be." You got this.

"*You've earned Penn, you deserve Penn,* and you have the right to put Penn and all that it offers to good use."

taking ownership

I will never forget the day I received my Penn acceptance.

Actually, it is probably more accurate to state the moment I received it—at the ripe old age of twenty-four, anything prior to my crazed refreshing of the application status web page is pretty blurry. I do remember feeling anxious all day at school, skipping the yearbook meeting and then rushing home to get on AIM and anxiously IM my friend Richelle—a Harvard hopeful and the only other Ivy League applicant in my friend group— until statuses were posted. But it only gets vividly memorable when I flash back to reading the few lines it took to confirm that I had been accepted.

My reaction was both physical and emotional. Six years later, and I still remember a hot, tingly face and swelling insides. And joy. Pure, boundless joy, which I expressed with out-loud laughter and an all-caps, virtual "I GOT IN!" scream to Richelle. I felt so proud and so empowered. I had chosen Penn, out of all of the other schools, as my dream school. I had visited the campus and filled out the application and written the personal statements and sat through the interview and gotten myself chosen by the only school I wanted to attend. A good school. A *selective* school. And although I had always been bright, and firmly occupied the "smart girl" niche at school, this made it official. Penn wasn't some tiny, all-girls' school tucked away in the Bronx. Penn was Ivy League. Penn engaged with smart people all over the world and still, Penn wanted me.

I probably could have flown that day. Had I not been distracted by my acceptance, I would have realized that I had sprouted wings and leapt off of the top of our garage.

Then I went to Penn, and never felt that way in all four years I was there. By this, I do not mean to communicate that my Penn experience was at all unfulfilling or disappointing. At Penn, I formed significant, life-enriching friendships that ended up teaching me more about myself than I could have anticipated. At Penn, I learned how to learn better—how to engage with subject matter more appreciatively and be grateful for the existence of knowledge and my ability to absorb it. At Penn, I found a distinct black community that had its great share of intelligent, talented, and interesting individuals—individuals to be inspired, comforted, and challenged by—and immersed myself in it. I sat in Sister Sister circles, starred in commercials for the BSL date auction, spent my Saturdays in Du Bois working with Ase's sixth and seventh grade contingent, and engaged with tiny native Philadelphians through CSSP.

I participated in enough endeavors and organizations to make me feel like I had made my time at Penn count. By the time graduation came around, I felt stretched and changed and mature. I felt proud and newly polished by my Penn degree.

But still, the total absence of that I-can-fly feeling over the course of those years was something that kept coming up as I struggled to figure out what I wanted to share with the Climbing Vines community. There was this question: Why, after four years in a place filled and bursting with opportunities and resources, had I not managed to do a special something that would have given me another dose of that empowered, take-flight feeling? And then the follow-up question: What could I have done differently to set myself up for one of those moments?

Writing this piece has been a study of these two questions, and while I am certain that the answer is multidimensional and far more complex than I can explain here, I do think the bottom line is that I never really took ownership of Penn. This idea stems from some advice that I heard along my college journey and, in retrospect, failed to implement. I never let myself feel as though I owned Penn—as though every last one of the opportunities and clubs and resources offered by the institution belonged to me. I very quickly found a comfort zone and said that's enough. And although that comfort zone did lead me to the significant and enriching experiences I outlined earlier, I think that venturing beyond that to try and succeed at something a little less familiar—like writing for *The F Word* or hosting a radio show or starting an extremely fun and unique a cappella group (shout out to my adventurous girlfriends!)—could have brought me closer to that elusive I-can-fly feeling. Penn belongs to me just as it belongs to everyone who has ever accepted the offer to spend his or her undergraduate years on this campus. I was told that early, but was a little late to believe it.

As I move further away from my college years, I am grateful for this opportunity to reflect on and pass down a snapshot of my own Penn experience. Writing this piece has unexpectedly led me to yet another life lesson, which just goes to show how much this institution can spark learning and invigorate the mind. To anyone who needs a reminder, please remember that Penn is yours—you've earned Penn, you deserve Penn, and you have the right to put Penn and all that it offers to good use.

contributors

Araba Ankuma C'17

Araba Ankuma, Ghanaian-bred and Virginia-born, graduated from the College of Arts & Sciences' unique Visual Studies program with a concentration in Fine Arts. Upon her departure from Penn, Araba established her company, ASA Productions, as the means through which to create, educate, and produce for those who seek greater visual literacy. Araba is currently living in Brooklyn, NY and pursuing a career as a creative director and producer.

Bahja Johnson W'12

Bahja Johnson, a native of St. Louis, Missouri, graduated from the Wharton School with a degree in Marketing and Legal Studies. She currently works in the retail industry in San Francisco, California. She loves exploring the city with friends, satisfying her inner foodie at new restaurants, and a great pair of heels.

Courtney Paul C'12

Courtney Paul, a native of The Bronx, New York, graduated from the College of Arts and Sciences with a degree in Psychology and minor in Hispanic Studies. She enjoys exploring Harlem, spending time with friends and family, reading fiction, and binge-watching TV shows on Netflix and Hulu.

Daina Troy W'98

Daina Troy, a native of Philadelphia, Pennsylvania, graduated from the Wharton School with a degree in Marketing and Entrepreneurial Management.

Jacqueline Baron C'13

Jacqueline Baron, a native of Alpharetta, Georgia, graduated from the College of Arts and Sciences with a degree in Psychology and minor in Sociology. She's currently a corps member of Teach for America in San Antonio, where she works as a Reading Intervention and AVID (College Readiness) teacher. In her spare time, she enjoys dancing, travelling, trying new restaurants, and spending time with her friends.

Janay Sylvester C'12

Janay Sylvester, a native of Seymour, Connecticut, graduated from the College of Arts and Sciences with a degree in PPE (Philosophy, Politics, and Economics). By day, she is a communications professional, by night she is an inspired creative — recording music, attending concerts, blogging, and following the latest media and entertainment news.

Janday Wilson C'10

Janday Wilson, a native of Ansonia, Connecticut, graduated from the College of Arts and Sciences with a degree in English, African American Literature concentration. Janday is a storyteller who respects and believes in the story inside of everyone, from the James Baldwins of the world to the VH1 reality stars.

Kalyne Coleman C'14

Kalyne Coleman, a native of Richmond, Virginia, graduated from the College of Arts and Sciences with a degree in Communication and minor in Theatre. Kalyne is currently pursuing her MFA in acting at the Actors Studio Drama School at Pace University in New York City. Coming to a stage or screen near you one day. ;) Just wait on it.

Kristie Gadson C'15

Kristie Gadson, a College of Arts and Sciences student from Ellenwood, Georgia, is pursuing her bachelor's degree in English concentrating in Literature, Journalism and Print Culture and a Fine Arts minor. She currently works as a program coordinator at the Kelly Writer's House. She enjoys writing short stories, drawing comics, and reading whatever books aren't required for class. She hopes to become an editor at a children's publishing agency when she graduates.

Mariama Diallo C'19

Mariama Diallo, a native of The Bronx, New York, graduated from the College of Arts and Sciences with a degree in Sociology with a concentration in Structures of Opportunity and Inequality, and a minor in Africana Studies. She is currently working towards her Masters of Social Work degree at the School of Social Policy and Practice within the University of Pennsylvania.

Morgan Roper C'10

Morgan Roper, a native of Los Angeles, California, graduated from the College of Arts and Sciences with a degree in English, Creative Writing concentration. Morgan lives in Brooklyn and works as the Production and Music Coordinator for the Nickelodeon series "Dora the Explorer" and the new spinoff, "Dora and Friends: Into the City." When she's not working, she's gallivanting around the city, trying new restaurants and bars, picnicking in the park, exploring her neighborhood (Park Slope!) and reading. She's the founder of an all-female book club, Babes on Books, and loves spending time with her fellow bookclub Babes!

Naeemah Philippeaux C'12

Naeemah Philippeaux, a native of Long Island, New York, graduated from the College of Arts and Sciences with a degree in English, Cinema Studies concentration, and minor in Fine Arts. Naeemah is a creative, dedicated thinker who is looking for the opportunity to improve the world using media technology and outside-the-box ideas. She is currently working at Google, trying to get more minorities into STEM (science, technology, engineering, and mathematics).

Nikki Hardison W'15

Nikki Hardison is a Wharton student from Atlanta, Georgia, pursuing a degree in Marketing. At Penn, she serves as Political Chair of the UMOJA Board, the new curator for *The Daily Pennsylvanian*'s "The Vision" column, and a member of the Gamma Epsilon Philadelphia City Chapter of Alpha Kappa Alpha Sorority, Incorporated.

Ruqayyah Malik C'15

Ruqayyah Malik, a College of Arts and Sciences student from Los Angeles, California, is pursuing a degree in Biology and minor in Chemistry. She was born in Lagos, Nigeria, and is the eldest of four children. She is completing her final undergraduate year at Penn and will be applying to medical school. She hopes to ultimately become a neurosurgeon. She enjoys knitting, reading, and making hilarious, side-splitting, foot-stomping, doubled-over-heaving-for-breath jokes.

Ruthie Hubbard C'12

Ruthie Hubbard, a native of Stamford, Connecticut, graduated from the College of Arts and Sciences with a degree in Communication and Marketing.

Sharree Walls C'13

Sharree Walls, a native of Chicago, Illinois, graduated from the College of Arts and Sciences with a degree in Urban Studies. Sharree is continuing the second year of the Fox Fellowship working at the YMCA in New Orleans. She enjoys yoga, running, and reading many books at one time.

Sonie (Guseh) Osagie C'10

Sonie Osagie, a native of Durham, North Carolina, graduated from the College of Arts and Sciences with a degree in English (concentration in Journalism and Print Culture) and a minor in Hispanic Studies. She currently works at CNBC in a role focused on content strategy, news partnerships, and business development. Sonie received her MBA in 2016 from Columbia Business School, and currently lives in Oakland, California, where she spends her free time reading inspirational memoirs, running at the lake, and visiting Wine Country.

Tamara Oki C'12

Tamara Oki, a native of Silver Spring, Maryland, graduated from the College of Arts and Sciences with a degree in History and African Studies with a French Studies minor. She is currently a Teach For America Recruitment Manager in Washington, D.C.

Victoria Ford C'15

Victoria Ford, a College of Arts and Sciences student from Greenville, South Carolina, is pursuing her bachelor's degree in English. She is a womanist, poet, and lover of words, barbecued foods, black proverbs, 90s cartoon theme songs, and social justice.

*All contributor bios from the first edition of Climbing Vines (pub. 2014) appear as is. They have been integrated with the bios of the new contributors to the second edition (pub. 2020) to maintain anonymity for all contributors.

acknowledgments

Climbing Vines GoFundMe campaign donors, the second edition of the collection exists only due to your support, we thank you.

Daina Troy, Michelle Houston, Dr. Brian Peterson, and the staff at Makuu Black Cultural Center for serving as an invaluable resource, we thank you.

Elisa Foster, Sherisse Laud-Hammond, and the staff at the Penn Women's Center for your contribution, we thank you.

CV Editorial Team (Victoria Ford & Ruani Ribe) for your creative influence, time, and counsel, I thank you.

Dad, Mom, and Franklin for being my biggest supporters and serving as my consulting team on every aspect of this project, I thank you.

www.ingramcontent.com/pod-product-compliance
Lightning Source LLC
Chambersburg PA
CBHW051426150726
48000CB00005B/1968